Sober Ever After

By

Jackie Elliott

Published by Writer Unblocked Publishing.

ISBN 978-0-9939542-2-1

Don't forget to Grab Some Free Resources!

If you enjoy this book, you can grab some free resources when you visit my website:

www.iamrunningonsober.com

Content

Introduction.

"I think we are well advised to keep on nodding terms with the people we used to be, whether we find them attractive company or not. Otherwise they turn up unannounced and surprise us, come hammering on the mind's door at 4 a.m. of a bad night and demand to know who deserted them, who betrayed them, who is going to make amends."
Joan Didion.

This book took far longer to write than I had intended.

In fact, it started off with a different, much catchier title, and I wrote the first draft quickly, with humour. I like humour. Even alcohol dependence can be funny right?

When I started editing however, it all sounded wrong. I sounded angry in the "funny" parts and far too flippant.

So I started again.

I didn't want this to be a "Dead Drunk in a Ditch on a Dark Night" kind of sober memoir. Not because it wouldn't have been captivating – everyone enjoys those kind of salacious details, and I probably would sell far more copies – but for this reason:

We humans are not so much "rational" beings, we are more "rational*izing*" beings.

When I was first flirting with sobriety, I would read sober memoirs, while sipping on my wine, reading rock bottom stories and *rationalizing to myself,*

"There's no way that I'm as bad as *that*"

I did behave badly. I did and said bad things and I hurt people. I was affected physically by my drinking. My bank account was definitely impacted, and I really pissed off a lot of people.

But my "rock bottom" is quite mundane compared to how thing *could* have turned out.

A few weeks into my sober quest, I was in hospital visiting a friend.

In the bed next to her, behind the curtains, I could hear a lady moaning and crying.

"She's detoxing" I was told.

This poor lady, while very drunk, had been mugged and beaten. She had ended up in hospital with several broken bones, and was going through her third detox.

It's a horrible process.

I saw no similarities in our situations at all.

I felt huge compassion for this lady, but I could not conceive that we *suffered from the same disease.*

And that's the problem.

"Alcoholism" at the very end of the spectrum, *is* actually a disease. A body that is completely addicted to booze, will, at some point, cease to function without it.

And then only medical intervention will be able to help, if at all.

I was not nearly at this stage. And most people, who have a nagging voice at the back of their mind, saying:

"I should really cut down on the wine"

They are not at that stage either.

And yet, the stereotypical image of an 'alcoholic' is identical to the lady in the hospital.

By that time, I had already committed to quitting.

I had tried for over three years to "moderate" and had failed. I broke all my self-imposed drinking rules on a regular basis, and slid back into my old habits.

But if I hadn't already known that a sober life was my best option, witnessing this poor lady would not have convinced me.

Only when I started blogging, did I find other sober bloggers whose stories resonated with me.

High functioning people who still got the kids to school on time, who still attended board meetings (albeit with hangovers), who still had marriages and houses and jobs. They all had "high bottoms".

Just like me.

This book was written to keep on "nodding terms" with my past self – it doesn't hurt, once in a while, to remind myself how far I've travelled – and also to make you, the reader, shuffle uncomfortably in your chair occasionally, if you recognise yourself.

If you are finding ways to rationalize drinking, like I did, *for decades*, then this is dedicated to you.

I hope this book makes you squirm. In the best possible way.

Love,

Jackie xx

Chapter 1 Worry Wart

Cognitive dissonance is the uncomfortable state of being caught between two conflicting desires. It's a psychological term, and when I came across it, I was filled with a sense of relief that there was an actual scientific explanation for a feeling that I was so accustomed to experiencing, it was practically my default emotion.

I knew it as merely *"being worried"*

A person with cognitive dissonance will make efforts to reduce the uncomfortable feeling.

There is no better way to temporarily achieve this reduction in cognitive dissonance, I've found, *than drinking your face off.*

Which I did, for much of my adult life.

No one likes to feel uncomfortable. No one enjoys worrying. No one relishes stress. No matter how many business gurus tell you that they 'thrive" on stress, I simply don't believe it.

I've always hated it. I've always longed to be one of those people who don't care what other people think, who let debt and drama slide off them. But I am not one of those people.

I am someone who worries about wearing the "right" clothes to social functions. Who worries about turning up on time, not embarrassing or humiliating myself in front of others, not laughing too loud at jokes, not breaking ANY of the rules, written or implied.

I once spent a whole night fretting and wishing I hadn't agreed to go fishing, because I had never stepped on a boat before, and what if it was too far from the dock? And what if I fell? Or I might be wearing the wrong shoes and slip on the deck, or if the sea was rough I might get sick, and what about holding a fishing rod? What if I dropped it and lost a fish?

Worrying is exhausting. And it was a relief to me that there was a magical liquid that could slowly dissolve away my default level of stress.

Settling down with a glass of wine every evening became a ritual that I relied on. The first sips of wine would seep into my soul. I felt comforted. I felt like I was in a warm, safe bubble where my troubles could not prod and poke at me.

The fretful monkey chatter in my brain receded. For a while, I stopped my world and got off.

I had nothing tangible to worry about.

I had the best childhood any person could hope for.

I had parents who fervently believed that their purpose in life was to create a better future for their two children, and to make the happiest memories possible, while they were going about that task.

When there was a shortage of money, my brother and I didn't know about it. If my parents were stressed, or "going through a rough patch", there was no impact on us.

Education was the Holy Grail. Both my parents, post war babies, proudly came from working class backgrounds, but aspired to be middle class, in white collar careers. secondary education was the goal for both of us.

Mum and Dad wanted to travel, wanted to own their own house, wanted a new car, and a comfortable retirement. And they worked for it.

Once a year we would go on our family summer holiday to Swanage. We stayed in the same guest house every year – The Craigendoran. It was a rambling old building, with room for about 20 families.

Most of us were escaping the City for the salt air and sandy beaches of the South Coast for two weeks of freedom from the "rat race"

We had the same room every year – all four of us together, with a tiny sink in the corner. No ensuite in those days – we had to time our shower in the shared bathroom to coincide with the hot water – and it was Bed and Breakfast only.

I still remember the aroma of fried bread and bacon in the morning, my Dad sneaking an extra greasy slice onto his plate

"I am on *holiday*, love" and winking at us kids, and afterwards we would walk to the beach, carrying buckets and spades, windbreakers, towels and swimming costumes. We would pause at the only tiny beach shop, and my brother and I would gaze at kites, inflatable boats, cheap trinkets and the ice cream counter...

"You've just had breakfast!"

And then we would arrive at our beach hut.

Musty, salty wooden huts in rows, rented for weeks at a time, the unspoken rule that the expanse of sand directly in front of the hut was "ours", so my dad would firmly stake our claim, by hammering in a wind break, and laying out our beach towels.

My mum would brew a pot of coffee over a tiny portable camp stove in that hut, and prepare lunch

'So much better to eat in the hut, we don't get the food all sandy."

And every day for two weeks, we would build sandcastles, play football on the beach, swim in the sea, pausing only to get reapplied with sunscreen, and our occasional trips to get ice cream cones.

If days were rainy, we would huddle in the hut, or trudge along the cliff walk to see the Old Harry Rocks, or visit Corfu Castle – not for the history lesson, but for the clotted cream teas served in the tiny 'Ye Olde Tea House".

I remember *all of this* because my parents worked hard for me to have these memories.

These days the Craigendoran is a nursing home, Swanage is a faded seaside town (maybe it always was?) and as we got older, our family got more adventurous with our travels, but those summers were *worry free for me.*

During one of my "moderation" attempts, I took up boxing.

I hoped that developing my fitness levels would somehow motivate me to drink less. And my fourteen year old granddaughter was exhibiting all the signs of "worry" that I recognised.

She was worried that she was too tall, too fat, not pretty enough, not popular enough. It stirred up old troublesome feelings inside of me, as I watched her struggle with make- up and try too hard to be friends with the "mean girls".

So we joined a boxing gym, and twice a week, for two agonizing hours, I was made to run, squat, pound on cement-like bags with large gloves, until every tiny cell in my body was shrieking for mercy.

While I hoped that this physical punishment would somehow rid my body of booze, like a sweaty exorcism, I also hoped that my granddaughter's confidence would be bolstered. If nothing else, she could pound her teenage anxiety and worry into a gym bag. I'm not sure if it worked, but she did get some amusement from seeing me in physical pain.

One Thursday night, she seemed more enthused to go than usual.

The reason was immediately apparent when we arrived at the gym.

He was pretty and he knew it. Short gelled hair, just the right amount of tan and stubble, impossibly white teeth, and as he carefully peeled off his sweatshirt, the type of sculpted muscles that are only achieved by narcissistic pumping in front of a mirror.

Sullen teenage girls melted into fawning puppies.

He leaned into the admiring gaggle, preening and savouring the moment. Just the brush of his hand on an arm, a knowing tilt of his chin, the merest perception of a glance in their direction, and I practically had to run over and catch them as they swooned and dropped like ninepins.

"Oh, Mr. Bradley", one of them managed to get a whole sentence out without a high pitched giggle, "Will you be coming every week?"

Mr. Bradley was a school teacher. Except when he was out of school it was 'Call me Mark"

Fucker.

The "cool teacher". Who somehow gets his rocks off by encouraging those teenage fantasies. Who thinks it isn't just OK to be their "friend" and dole out hugs, and let them cross all boundaries, it is *his reward,* the "perk" of the job.

My "Call me Mark" was one of the "cool" teachers. He would laugh and joke with the boys, occasionally take a drag of their cigarettes behind the Horticultural buildings, and once he caused a stir of excitement when he left a copy of Playboy on his desk.

I was in love.

He was really careful not to actually *touch me* until I was sixteen. Up until then, it was just discreet hand holding, quick hugs and meetings after school for "extra tuition".

My "Call me Mark", like all of the men (and sometimes women) who abuse their power over children, was a predator, who bolstered his own self esteem by feeding into my teenage confusion and loneliness.

It was over quickly.

The School Board fired "Call me Mark" and offered counselling to me, the victim. Except I didn't feel like a victim, I felt like one half of a tragic love story.

My parents were devastated.

I screamed and cried and pleaded.

I recall one evening as my Dad poured himself a large whiskey, took a deep breath, and tried to question me as gently as possible, whilst containing his rage, coaxing all the details that no father ever wants to hear.

As I told him, crying, I watched as he sipped his whiskey. It seemed to calm him a little.

Hours later, when the murmur of anxious and angry voices from my parent's bedroom, finally died down, I crept downstairs.

I poured myself a glass of whiskey.

I sat in the darkness, and sipped. I gradually calmed down enough to go back to bed and sleep.

Until then I barely noticed alcohol.

I have a few memories of my parents staggering in from PTA dances, giggling and slamming doors too loudly.

My mum put on the kettle when she came in from work, and she occasionally had a sweet sherry with Sunday Dinner.

At Christmas Time, my Nan would wink at my brother and me and make us a 'Snowball" of foamy Advocaat and lemonade – disgusting, but we gagged it down, because we were "drinking with the grown- ups".

Wine made its debut at our dinner table in the early 1980's.

Mrs. Thatcher was Prime Minister, the country was hopeful that the austere 1970's with blustering Union leaders having beer and sandwiches at Downing Street were over, and finally there seemed to be more cash in people's pockets. It was a few years before "Loadza money!" was the cry from the barrow boys of the Stock Exchange, but everyone was getting used to having more and spending more.

Wine wasn't flowing, but it was more common to see a bottle of Blue Nun or Liebfraumilch replacing the sherry on Sunday.

Like all teenagers I experimented.

I didn't like beer, but I could hold down a fair amount of cheap cider.

I never really thought that I could hold my booze. I always seemed to get drunker quicker, and vomit sooner than all my peers.

"Because you drank so much more than all of us" said one old school friend incredulously when I mentioned this at a reunion years later.

Even then I knew that I drank *differently*.

I drank to blot out anxiety.

After "Call me Mark" had disappeared from my life, I still had to endure all the whispers and pointing. I had "celebrity" status and was invited to all the parties, only to discover that the boys thought that I would be easy, and the girls wanted to hear all the lurid details.

I drank whatever alcohol I could get my hands on, and inevitably arrived home, drunk and crying.

'Alcohol and you don't mix", Dad said to me one morning, after finding me covered in my own vomit, passed out in the bathroom.

Twenty years ago, I visited Italy with my then-boyfriend.

The fuzzy glow on our relationship was already beginning to fade, and in the same way that tired dispirited couples often plan babies or big weddings to paper over the cracks in the relationship, we had instead decided to move to a different country.

I had my own dream, that I had spent my lifetime chasing, which involved shady olive groves, living off goat's milk and lush vegetables from our own garden and laughter-filled afternoons as I canned tomatoes and practiced my broken Italian with the elders of the village. I imagined that once we shed all the baggage of modern life, the debt, the endless consumption, the stress about the insignificant, we could reclaim the first heady days of being in love.

My boyfriend made it very clear that he didn't intend to spend the rest of his life squeezing olives.

The trip was a disappointment.

After two weeks of bickering and sweating in the heat, wandering round half ruined farm cottages with no proper sanitation and antiquated wiring, my dream was tarnished and our relationship was further strained. We headed to Rome for a couple of days.

With the pressure off, we actually managed to relax in Rome (we were both far more comfortable with the relentless impersonal busy-ness of City life), and we wandered around the chaotic mix of historic ruins, haute culture, and sundrenched plazas.

The last day, we found a tiny restaurant with seating for about six at battered formica tables. It was empty, except for a tiny wizened Senora, who beckoned us in, and then circled round us, as if herding us into her establishment.

We shrugged, obeyed and then listened to an incomprehensible tirade of Italian from the Senora, before she disappeared for about twenty minutes behind a grimy plastic curtain.

We waited, in awkward silence as a dirt encrusted air-conditioner unit wheezed out lukewarm air, and dripped on the floor, forming the only clean patch.

Our apprehension about possible food poisoning (heightened, as we had a day's travelling scheduled to start the following morning), evaporated like the steam and aroma that rose from two dishes of fresh pasta that emerged from behind the curtain, carried by The Senora.

To uneducated English eyes, it looked as though she had forgotten to top the pasta (we were so accustomed to piles of flavourless fat and protein that usually suffocated our spaghetti dinners), but as we twisted and sampled exquisite strands drenched in oil, the flavours danced on our taste buds.

It made us smile.

Senora poured two glasses of red wine from a glass jug.

The wine warmed us. Hints of summer fruit, ripening in dappled sunshine, slowed down time in that shabby café, and we laughed together.

For a short while, as I let the alcohol work its magic, I found myself believing that it was still possible to fix love, and my dreams were within my grasp.

We spend so much rummaging around in our past, looking for trauma and tragedies, inherited traits and flawed genes to somehow explain our bond to booze, that most of the time, we overlook the Big Con.

The human species has been getting wasted since one bright spark decided to drink the putrid juice of rotting fruit – just for the fun of it, to see what it tasted like, the same way that kids try to lick steel telephone poles when it's freezing – and chanced upon the intoxicating effects of ethanol.

Imagine what an afternoon that must have been...

Since then, alcohol (despite the millennia of hangovers and tiny detail that the liquid is *toxic to the human body*), booze has been a cultural icon.

We drink to celebrate births, birthdays, marriages, kids, divorce, new jobs, retirement and death.

This is not the problem for me or many other drinkers. The real problem isn't the glass of fizz and sparkles for the new bride, or the warm, convivial glass of brandy on Christmas Eve. It isn't even the odd riotous teenage party where cheap cider and dusty bottles of Ouzo stolen from the liquor cabinet inevitably end up as vomit and promises 'to never drink again'.

These rite of passage don't cause the cognitive dissonance of misery and compulsion that all dysfunctional drinkers experience, as the love affair with booze moves into the acrimonious divorce stage.

No, the big problem, is that we *depend on* booze. It's not a celebratory toast, or a weekend social, or even the punctuation of the end of the work day – it's the continuous use of booze as a prop in our lives.

Stress at work? *I need a drink.*

Argument with the sister in law? *Pour another glass.*

General disappointment with your perceived lifelong underachievement? *There's a wine for that.*

Dysfunctional drinkers, alcoholics, we all depend on booze to "fix" whatever it is on our lives that causes us pain or disappointment.

I learned that at an early age.

It wasn't the emotional trauma that I was going through, it wasn't that my life was any more pressured or stressed than anyone else, it was just that I found out that alcohol provided a relief, however temporary, from whatever ailed me.

The Alcohol Industry is on to it. Hell, they practically invented it!

Back in the Eighties, woman were not significant consumers of booze. This posed a problem for the Alcohol Industry who viewed women as an untapped segment of the marketplace.

It wasn't so much that women "underperformed" as far as the

Industry was concerned, they figured out that collectively, we didn't really have any reason to drink, beyond the social and celebratory. *Or at least, we weren't aware yet there should be any other reason....*

We needed to be informed and educated.

Like snake oil salesmen, the Alcohol Industry hasn't been pushing the "sexiness" of booze, it's found a much more effective hook; the "restorative power" of wine.

More troubling than the direct advertising of smooth Merlots and buttery Chardonnays sipped by impossibly beautiful and sophisticated women, is the suggestive portrayal of the same sophisticated professionals uncorking a bottle at the first sign of a hurdle or a challenge.

More dangerous than images of women drinking beer round camp fire, chinking glasses of wine at the Girl's Night Out, or sipping

thoughtfully at the weekly book club –
although these commercials are
intensely annoying to anyone who
has now figured out that life's fun
moments are not dependent on the
beverage – no, the more insidious
images are those that you see on
social media now. These are the
comic pictures of "The Winebulance",
the 'Mum memes" suggesting that
parenting is not only easier with wine,
but almost impossible without it, the
drip, drip, drip of the narrative that
every problem, every stressful event
in your life...*is made better by booze.*

That the Big Con. I fell for it. That's
how I was drinking.

I rarely got drunk at a social
functions. I may have been boorish,
rude and repeated myself a lot, but I
didn't fall over, or start fights, or
vomit (well, not often)

At the end of the evening, I would
mostly stop and get another bottle of
wine, and drink it until I passed out.
Alone.

And that's the subtle shift in drinking patterns from my consumption, compared to my mum's generation.

I once asked her why she didn't drink when my brother and I were children.

"But I did drink", she said "As soon as you were old enough to be left with a babysitter, I went to all your Dad's functions. And we had people over for dinner all the time"

No, I said, why didn't you drink every day? When you came home from work?

"What on earth for?" she asked, genuinely confused.

There's the difference. It's not so much that alcohol is any more "normal" (although it is), or that women have been lead to believe that drinking somehow is badge of feminism, a way to keep up to the boys (although many women do believe that), it's not that we have more disposable income or more independence – all of these facts have influenced our drinking patterns, but *the one single factor* that makes one woman's fun, another woman's downwards ride on the alcoholism elevator – is WHY we drink.

For my mum, drinking was a social event, enjoyed with my Dad at the end of the day, or to enhance the ambience of a social gathering.

For me, it was a solo event.

Years after my first sip of whiskey, alone in the dark, and the trip to Rome, I was in another country, just after another failed relationship, and because I couldn't figure out the sense of it all, or put the fragments of my life into any recognisable order, I did what I knew best. I drank.

My mum phoned me.

"Don't drink alone" she said,

"Mum, I answered. *If I didn't drink on my own, I wouldn't drink at all*"

Chapter 2 Am I an Alcoholic?

The first time I asked myself that question, I had a hangover (of course) which I was trying to quell with an Egg McMuffin and a milky coffee. I was standing on the side of the street, waiting to see a local celebrity jog past holding the Olympic Torch.

The night before, I was staying with my friend C, we had a heated discussion about whether the Winter Olympics were more exciting than the Summer Olympics (I remember the discussion), and then we made the decision to haul our asses out of bed early on a chilly January morning to stand, hopping from one foot to another, watching the parade of civic pride and a glimpse of the Olympic Flame before it made its way to

Vancouver for the Winter Games, 2010.

I didn't recall that part of the discussion. I didn't recall wrapping my dog in a blanket and putting him to bed like a small child, because apparently I was incoherent with grief over yet another failed relationship, I didn't recall C stroking my hair, and comforting me. And I certainly didn't recall agreeing to get up in the morning to watch the parade. Because I hate parades.

I literally didn't remember any of it....and I still don't.

I woke up with my eyes feeling really grainy, and my dog whining to go out for a pee. I stumbled into the living room and counted the empty bottles of wine. I tried to reconcile the extent of my hangover to the proportion of wine that I had consumed *myself* from the eight empty bottles. Unfortunately, I couldn't remember how many people had been drinking with me.

A quick count of stained glasses would indicate four people in total.......

"I guess we really tied one on....?" I half joked and half asked, when C emerged from her bedroom.

"You don't remember *anything at all?*"

Nope. I really didn't.

I passed it off as a one-time incident. After all, I had been through a break-up in my long term relationship, my then boyfriend was still married to someone else and looked like remaining that way, and the income from my less than illustrious career in Real Estate was barely covering my mortgage.

I needed a big blow-out like last night. It did me good to get it all out. Maybe the alcohol was a helpful release valve.

But the total memory loss bothered me.

Isn't that something that only happens to Alcoholics?

Fast forward five years, and I feel like I have an unofficial Master's Degree in Alcoholism, dysfunctional drinking, brain damage, and yes, why it is that I can't remember that particular evening, and so many others over the last five years.

Am I an Alcoholic? I have asked myself that a thousand times, and attempted to find the answer by completing online questionnaires, reading sober memoirs, self- help books, sober blogs and then writing my own blog and creating my OWN website...to try and help the many other people out there who are asking themselves the same question, over and over.

And the answer?

I still don't know. But the question has become largely irrelevant.

What I've discovered is this:

If you think you MIGHT be an alcoholic......you *probably do* have a drinking problem.

As soon as you figure this out, be prepared for everything you THINK you know about alcohol, alcoholics and getting sober, to be completely turned on its head.

The problem is that the warning signs of alcohol abuse (although apparent to everyone else) are hard for a drinker to spot, and even if we do, *we go into immediate denial.*

Complete memory loss should have been a warning flag for me, but it wasn't. The inability to give a shit about my job or my financial situation should have been a warning flag, but it wasn't. The complete lack of morality on my behalf, as I continued an affair with a Married Man, should have been a warning flag but it wasn't.

But I was lucky.

Firstly, I was lucky enough to meet someone who *still has* complete faith in me, even when I don't deserve it, and secondly, he met me and grabbed me off the downwards sliding Alcohol Elevator before I hit the bottom floor.

I hope that if you are reading this book, and you have this vague anxious feeling that *maybe your drinking is out of control........maybe you are an alcoholic,* then some of my experiences, both during my years of Magical Drunken Thinking, and then my subsequent "recovery" will help you pinpoint whether or not you have a problem and give you a few pointers about what you can do about it.

I have to tell you though, that unless you picked up a copy of this book, which was left on the train, and you're only flicking through it because you have *nothing else whatsoever to do...*if you are experiencing that vague feeling of anxiety in the pit of your stomach, every time you think about your drinking, *then you do have a problem.*

Oh no, I hear you say. I do worry about my health and everything, but I'm not really a big drinker.....

First Sign That Your Drinking is a Problem – You Are A Habitual Bullshitter.

All drinkers are bullshitters. We have to be, to cover up our drinking. Unfortunately, the bullshit tends to invade other parts of our life (and the drinking does too) so we start to exist in this perpetual fraudulent state.

I hung up my Real Estate Licence, having been fired for a very embarrassing incident and I borrowed some money, and started a bookkeeping business. I rented a large office, and put tasteful pictures on the wall, plants on the shiny office furniture, and a welcoming sign.

Clients came in, I was plausible, they were won over by my expensive office and calming British accent, and reassured by my "solid" banking background. They thanked me. "You are a lifesaver", they said, "What would we do without you?" I lapped it up. (*Alcoholics aren't lifesavers now, are they? See?*)

The boxes of receipts and bank statements started flowing in. At first I worked for hours and hours, (well, I worked some hours, until about Wine O'Clock) but then I started to panic – there was no way that I could cover the rent for my office AND my apartment....AND pay for my car, my groceries, my phone bill (wine bill)......LET ALONE be SUCCESSFUL!! Be the competent, efficient, GREAT bookkeeper that existed only in my imagination and the faith of my duped clients.

I started making excuses to myself "if only I had better software", and then still worse, I made excuses to my clients. I had imaginary flu, fake family emergencies, my car broke down....it was endless, and as the outraged and bewildered clients grabbed their boxes and left, my bank account dwindled as quickly as a chilled bottle of chardonnay on a summer's afternoon.

Not only was I a failure, but a liar and a fraud. And a Bullshitter.

Worse than being a bullshitter, is being a bullshitter who believes her own bullshit.

Driving home one night, after sharing a (large) bottle of wine with a friend, I convinced myself that I was OK to drive.

I left it too late to brake before a sharp bend on a deserted country road. My car flew off the tarmac and settled in a ditch. The airbags immediately went off, and the car filled with smoke. Stunned, but not hurt, I managed to get the door open and I scrambled through the undergrowth, and sat on the side of the road, shaking and sobbing.

I knew I would be in trouble if I called the police. I was fairly certain that if I blew into a breathalyser I would be over the limit.

So I walked home. I went straight to bed and fell into a blackout sleep.

The noise from the TV pulled me back into consciousness. I got up and stumbled around trying to find the remote control. Then I realized that the TV was off. I saw lights through the crack in my bedroom curtains. Then I knew I was screwed. The police had arrived.

Of course, shortly after my car plunged into the ditch, and I had started trudging home, a Good Samaritan had caught a glimpse of my stranded vehicle in the undergrowth and had called the police.

My bullshit saved me. *For once.*

"I swerved to miss a deer" I explained..."And I wasn't hurt, so I thought I would just call a tow truck in the morning.......It's lovely of you to be so concerned, I am *so sorry* to have caused anyone *any* inconvenience.."

The police officers didn't look convinced, but filed a report and gave me a number....and within twelve hours, I was recounting the *same bullshit* to the Insurance Clerk....and by now, was starting to feel OUTRAGE towards the imaginary deer.

Second Sign That Your Drinking is a Problem....You Stop Being an Adult.

For the short time that I did function as bookkeeper, I was often visited by fellow drunkards (it takes a drunk to spot a drunk) with boxes or garbage bags full of receipts, which they expected me to make sense of within twelve hours, and then complete ten years of tax returns, so they could avoid whatever harsh penalty the frustrated Tax Officer was threatening that particular week.

I heard all manner of excuses Heart attacks (either themselves/spouse/dearest friend), bitchy ex-wife took all their papers, dog ate the bank statements...and I listened respectfully, nodding my head, pretending to believe every word...because even bullshitters have a sense of comradery, right?

Also, I knew exactly how these situations occurred, because *I hadn't done my tax returns for years either!*

In a rare moment of honestly and self- awareness, one client said to me.

"Nearly every evening I *intended* to sort these receipts out....but it was always easier to open another bottle of wine"

Absolutely. I knew exactly what he meant.

It was always easier to open another bottle of wine than to pay bills on time, fill in census forms, call my parents, get my eyes tested, get the car serviced, or do any of the mundane duties that fall on your lap when you become an adult.

Third Sign That Your Drinking is a Problem........You are always Waiting.

Waiting for someone or something to save you. Waiting for your drinking to stop magically on its own, or at least be under control...

"Don't worry" I would tell my dog as I poured another glass of wine (it's not drinking alone if you have a pet) "This is HAPPY drinking"

But I was rarely *happy* when I was drinking. I had moments of pleasure, obviously, and I really did love drinking, but I wasn't *happy.* I was always *waiting* to be happy.

It's like sitting at a bus stop for your entire life. Not a pretty bus stop in the countryside where you can see fields and flowers and hear the birds sing; *No*, a dull grey municipal bus stop, where all you have to do to pass the time is read and re-read the bus timetable, and although you could leave, you can't muster up the energy, and anyway, you are fairly certain that the bus will be along anytime soon.....and you'll be magically transported off to happiness and success and achievement....

Miraculously, while I was waiting, a Bus (sent from the Universe, I believe, as a type of *test* to see if I was worth bothering with) dropped off my husband.

Luckily, I looked up from my wine glass long enough to realise that something truly magical had happened. And I shouldn't fuck it up.

Of course, if I had quit drinking right then, this book would be extremely short. And would convey the entirely wrong message...

"Woman drinks too much and screws up her life. She waits for a miracle, gets one and stops drinking. The end"

It was a bit more involved than that. And before I got to the happy ending bit, I had to go through some shit, and sadly, I put other people through it too.

People who drink, tell you what they think you want to hear. And for the first year of my marriage, I did exactly that. My husband was mistakenly under the impression that I was *far more fun than I actually was, far more successful, far smarter, and far more reliable.*

In the middle of the Mojave Desert, California, turn left off Route 58 onto Highway 352, and you will pass a billboard, jammed into dusty patch of scrubland that reads;

"Welcome to Adelanto! The City of Unlimited Possibilities!"

The brave optimism of this grandiose proclamation becomes apparent as you drive for another half an hour, passing only vacant parking lots and seemingly unoccupied trailers surrounded by discarded appliances and rusty, wheel-less trucks balanced precariously on cement blocks and are secured only by impenetrable brambles.

If the optimism seems misplaced once you've viewed the outskirts of the "city" then the "downtown" area does nothing to reverse this opinion.

Every other store is boarded up, the sidewalks seem deserted, even the obligatory Walmart is desolate.

Adelanto (meaning "progress" in Spanish) was established in 1915, by Earl Richardson who invented the Hot Point Iron. He hoped to sell parcels of land to settlers, but the area never really took off. Over the decades, despite being incorporated as a City in 1970, just about three quarters of Adelanto is still bare desert.

Adelanto has been beset by financial woes. Poverty rates are high, city amenities have been stripped to the bone, even the High School remains half built. The only source of income is a paltry dollar per day for each inmate in the Prison Facility that the City sold off to raise cash.

The City declared a fiscal emergency just weeks before we arrived.

My new husband and I drove through Adelanto on our way to Phoenix Arizona.

At first, I was amused at the audacity of the Billboard. What possibilities could there exist here, in this dusty, derelict City, on the verge of being swallowed back into the desert?

But for some reason, that Billboard remained in my mind for the rest of trip and prompted me, months later to do some research. Did the City still exist?

This was the trip where my own cracks were starting to show. This was the trip where I learned that words are meaningless unless they are accompanied by action.

This was the trip when it was apparent that my continuous denial that I had a drinking problem was as disingenuous as that Billboard, and that my Bullshit was as apparent as the hopelessness of the city.

Three times on that trip, I got hopelessly drunk. I never intended to, of course. I always intended to have *just one glass.*

One morning, I woke up alone in a hotel room in Phoenix. It took me a while to get orientated.

"Where am I?" I panicked for a moment, then remembered. We were here on a business trip. I was here to help my husband get his marketing material together. To get his notes in order, to prepare his sale pitch.

When was the big meeting? Today.

I waited all day in the hotel room for my husband to return.

I'll never drink again. I'll never let him down again. I'll be better. I'll be better. I'll be better.

He was jubilant, the meeting was great! He hadn't needed the notes. I hadn't screwed up. Let's get wine! Let's drink to the future!

I poured a large glass for both of us.

To celebrate our unlimited possibilities.

It would take me three more years before I figured out that my "possibilities" were being severely limited by my drinking.

Chapter 3 Drunken Magical Thinking

I know how to eliminate Drunk Driving for good.

It would be easy, effective and relatively inexpensive. It would save countless lives. And it could be implemented *really quickly.*

All we need to do is to get car manufacturers to install an ignition breathalyser in every car. The car would not start unless the person with the key has passed the breathalyser test.

The benefits of this are 1. The technology already exists and is proven 2. It doesn't cost much and could be subsidised by a Government tax break from all the tax dollars saved from extra police officers and useless drunk driving campaigns showing severed limbs to completely desensitised audiences who see *far worse* on the local evening news. It just requires the will of the people and government to pass new legislation.....and voila! Safe roads for everyone!

But it won't be done. And do you know why?

Firstly, the alcohol industry will get its BIG GUNS out, and secondly,

Some bleeding hearts liberal focus group (funded by the Alcohol Industry) will whine and snivel about how it encroaches on civil liberties and how governments should not "punish" people before they have done something wrong. Conservative groups, equally funded, will point to "individual responsibilities" and the elimination of "Big Government" and the "Nanny" state.

But this is complete BOLLOCKS. And do you know why?

Because people who drink alcohol, intending to drive home (believing that they are "under the limit") *need to be punished in advance.*

"Normal" sober people are shocked at the thought of getting into a car and driving drunk.

Some "normal' people are able to drive to a pub, drink one glass of wine and then drive home, well under the limit, posing no threat to anyone.

Other people (like me), are also shocked at the thought of getting into a car and driving drunk. People (like me) NEVER EVER intend to drive drunk.

But People Like Me, also only ever intend to have one glass of wine. And then People Like Me have another one (because they had a large dinner, and this will be the last one, I'll have water after this and a bag of crisps, just to be on the safe side)

And then People Like Me have another "half a glass" (because the glasses of wine are waaaayy smaller in a pub, so really I've only drunk one 'biggish' glass, and I'm used to drinking far more than this. I have a bag of nuts and a glass of water to make sure)

This is Drunken Magical Thinking.

Drunken Magical Thinking flies under the radar. It sneaks up on you. It comes disguised as Completely Rational Logic, and it cannot be spotted or stopped until it has wreaked its havoc. Until the damage is done. Until lives are ruined.

You have to stop it before it starts.

*"**Hi honey**, how was your day? I'll get some dinner warmed up for you"*

Inaudible reply.

"Geez, they're really working you hard on this deal, aren't they?"

Muffled sound of kissing....'Go get a shower..."

A warm comfortable exchange between married people. *Happily married people.*

Except I was listening in to my boyfriend and his supposedly estranged wife, via a pocket-dialled cell phone call, about half an hour after he had left *my house.*

Of course, that was the immediate end of the relationship.

He was married and what kind of man cheats on his wife? *What kind of women betrays the sisterhood by having an affair with a married man? Even if he has sworn undying love and promised to divorce his wife as soon possible (probably next year, as long as his oldest finishes college, he doesn't want to 'unsettle" his children, and then of course, he has elderly parents....but as soon as ALL THIS is cleared up......we'll be together forever. Because he loves me. I make him feel "alive again")*

But now, having eavesdropped on this conversation, it's clear that the marriage that was "over" a decade ago and the "cold stand-offish" wife who "practically leads her own life", and "only shares the same house for convenience"..........*didn't get the memo.*

So the logical course of action was to finish the relationship immediately. I had been lied to. I was enabling a man to commit adultery, and I was at least partially responsible for the breaking of marriage vows. I had become a Mistress. The Other Woman. So I should finish it *right now.*

Except I didn't.

I turned the phone off. I ignored the text that I received an hour later....

"Hey, I called you by mistake. Sorry, I was still working. I'll see you tomorrow, xoxo"

Fucking liar.

I drank a bottle of red wine that night. Ironically, he (Married Man) had left it for me, it was called "Therapy"

We'll drink it together, he said, "*next time I'm over for dinner*"

But I drank it alone. It was Therapeutic.

As the man shuffled nearer to the counter, I noticed two things. First, his teeth were brown and stained as he grimaced at me (an attempt at a smile, I hoped) and second, the invisible smog of odour, so dense that I could actually *taste it,* hit me first, a good three feet before his actual body caught up.

I gripped the counter, so that I wouldn't step back.

"What can I do for you?" I asked as cheerily as possible.

I couldn't part my lips too far, in case I gagged and vomited.

The man lent towards me.

I gripped harder.

"Lucky"

No I'm fucking not, I thought, otherwise I wouldn't be here right now.

"Beg your pardon?"

"Lucky! Lucky! Lucky!" The grimace wasn't a smile. It had turned into a threatening sneer.

"*What the fuck....*"

"He wants a large can of cold Lucky Beer, don't you, Phil?"

Rhonda (the Rodent, as I had named her) came to my rescue, finally, her little rat face contorted as she tried not to laugh...

"Phil collects cans along the side of the road, and trades them for a Nice Cold Lucky Beer, don't you Phil?" she practically coo'd.

Phil was one of the regulars at the Beer and Wine Store where I was forced to moonlight after the Real Estate market had come crashing down. I had failed to sell *a single house,* after my exceptionally lazy lawyer had persuaded me to take a paltry divorce settlement deal.

'You're still young! You can make that money back again in no time! No need for any further unpleasantness..."......over his shoulder as he speedily exited the office before I could argue, and he missed his Tee Time...

So I was broke. Working the night shift with Rhonda the Rodent at the local Beer and Wine Store. And now I had met one of the "characters" who frequented the store on a regular basis.

The owner of the store, Daryl was an obnoxious little man, who made up for his lack of height with a callous indifference to his staff and clients.

Don't ever refuse to serve anyone...he warned....if they are really drunk, just make sure they are out of the parking lot, then we're not liable.

I was both fascinated and repulsed by the customers.

Stinky Phil was just one of a small army of homeless people who had carved a profitable "niche" career out of collecting empty pop and beer cans, and trading them for more alcohol.

Every three hours or so, one of them would arrive, with several cans neatly arranged in a cardboard box, Rhonda would calculate the recycling fee, and then "pay" them with single chilled cans of Lucky Beer.

Daryl had discovered that his profit margin on one can of beer increased by 400% if he broke up a case of beer, and sold the cans separately. And added a "chill charge".

Rhonda the Rodent explained. "We don't make money from people just buying a couple of bottles of wine every weekend. We make money from the *regular drinkers.*"

'What happens when they die? Won't the cash flow dry up?

"Oh no" she said, missing my sarcasm, "This is a welfare town.

There are always regular drinkers to keep us afloat"

Welfare Wednesday was our busiest evening.

Flush with cash (Daryl always obligingly cashed welfare cheques for a percentage charge) the *regular drinkers* celebrated every second Wednesday, sometimes "treating" themselves with a few cans of Stella Artois (*the alcohol content is higher, Rhonda explained, they get their buzz quicker*), and we were busy escorting stumbling human beings to the edge of the parking lot. Some of them were so drunk, that they urinated as they staggered, and I had to be careful that I wasn't splashed.

So we weren't *liable.*

"You have to tell her" I texted. 'It's not fair. The sooner she knows, the sooner we can all move on"

This had become my daily mantra to Married Man.

I cajoled, pleaded, cried and eventually, after a bottle of wine, became demanding and manipulative.

"I'll just tell her myself! Why should I be a liar too? You've turned me into a liar! I'm going to tell her tomorrow if you don't"

It had become a tedious pattern.

He would text back at first furious and then placating....

"You know I love you. Just be patient a little while longer. We'll make a plan. Tomorrow"

And I, afraid that I would lose him, poured another glass of wine, and wept, knowing that there would be no plan. Not tomorrow. Not ever.

The lady must have sensed me watching, because she looked up and asked,

"Have you ever tried this wine? Do you know what it's like?"

She was browsing in the dustier section of the Beer and Wine Store. Imported wines from the USA.

(*Only 18% mark-up, Rhonda told me. Try to steer them to the domestic section*)

"No, I haven't. But it's a great label, and that's how I choose my wine!" *Fuck you, I told Rhonda in my 'inside voice"*

"Well, I've give it a go!" the lady said, smiling, "And I'll let you what it's like!"

She came back the next day.

"It was lovely, it went really well with a roasted leg of lamb". She smiled a lot I noticed.

"I'll try another bottle!" She bought two.

A couple of days later she returned.

She bought three bottles of the same red wine, and two cheap bottles of white.

"To cook with!" She said, as she saw me looking at her purchases.

"You're having a dinner party?" I asked.

"Oh, I have a weekly get-together with the girls, I cook and we try new wines. Every Friday. Without fail."

"Sounds awesome". It really did. My culinary efforts went as far as toast, paired with whatever cheap wine I could afford.

I never had time to eat properly. I was still attempting to hold together my Real Estate "career" by day, and Beer and Wine Store cashier by night. Having time to eat was a luxury.

"Julia Childs" as I called her, became a regular, but not the urine –stained variety. She chatted about her Friday Night dinner parties, and gave me cooking and wine pairing tips that I would never use, because, well, all wine goes with toast.

But she was a welcome interlude between the haggard, beaten down "Stinky Phil" crowd that we usually served. With a smile.

'You drink a lot of wine" Rhonda the Rodent remarked, as I grabbed a bottle at the end of my shift.

"Er, not really".

"Well, you get a bottle almost every day"

"I don't think so", I smiled pleasantly and inwardly was pounding her rat features with the litre of Merlot that I had under my arm.

"Oh yes", she smirked, 'You're almost a *regular drinker* now"

Fuck her. Now I would have to buy my wine from the Government Liquor Store.

I finished my shift at 11, was home by 11.30, and these days, I was skipping the toast, just pouring a large glass of wine, letting the dog out to pee, and heading to bed, after checking for texts or messages from Married Man.

Most mornings, I would wake up to the acrid smell of stale wine from the glass next to my bed, to accompany my regular morning sweaty hangover.

I would shower and brush my teeth multiple times, paranoid that I smelled like Stinky Phil, ever since Married Man had commented that I "smelled like a brewery".

My financial situation wasn't improving either.

My Real Estate Listings were dwindling. Most of my clients had taken their business elsewhere, because they were frustrated that I rarely returned phone calls, and when I did, the whole conversation would be in rushed whispers, as I tried to duck down behind the shelves of wine, or hide out in the walk –in-fridge.

It was futile. Every month, the Real Estate board would charge a monthly fee, the office would charge a desk fee, I would fail to sell a house, and the debt would pile up.

Finally, Karma made the decision for me.

As I arrived for my evening shift at the Beer and Wine Store, one Welfare Wednesday night, my cell phone vibrated.

I had been summoned to the Real Estate office.

"I've got to go for an hour" I told Rodent. She was counting out Stinky Phil's empties, while he and half a dozen of his drunken cronies were peeing their pants and jostling around the Lucky Beer Cooler.

"You can't" she hissed, "I have a store full of regulars!"

I went anyway.

When I got there, one of my last remaining clients was in the office with my Manager.

I tried to be cheerful.

"Hi there! What's up?"

My client handed me a piece of paper.

'We received this in the mail, this morning"

It was a picture of me. It had been cut out of the Real Estate Weekly flyer, and taped to another piece of paper.

Underneath, in block capitals, like a child's art and craft project, the anonymous author had written;

SLUT! ADULTERESS! FORNICATOR! HOME WRECKER!

'You've been fired"

Rhonda the Rodent greeted me cheerfully, as I arrived for my shift the following day.

I didn't give a shit.

I had already handed in my Real Estate licence. My manager was sympathetic, but firm.

"We can't have this kind of bad publicity, it's a small town"

I threatened Married Man that I was taking the Adulteress Flyer to the police.

"This is from your wife. It's a threatening letter. I shall have her charged"

He was horrified. I watched him squirm for a while, just for my own amusement and revenge, and then shredded the note, followed by our relationship.

Then I went to the Government Liquor Store and grabbed two large bottles of cheap wine off the shelf. No fucking way was I going to spend my last fifty bucks in Daryl's store, and give Rhonda an opportunity to smirk at me.

As I waited in line to pay, I heard a familiar voice;

"'I love this wine, thank you for recommending it"

It was "Julia Childs", my lovely Gourmet Chef friend.

She had a two large bottles of red wine, and one bottle of white.

"The white wine is for cooking, I have my regular weekly dinner party tonight. Just me and the girls, every Thursday Night. Without fail"

Drunken Magical Thinking can take a stranglehold on your life. Slowly, but surely, completely rational people behave in bizarre ways that no one else can fathom, seduced by Booze.

It's like all those news reports about stupid greedy people, mesmerized by the promise of a million dollars from a Nigerian Prince, *if they will only help out by sending all the details of their bank account right now.....*people shake their head and ask "why on earth would they do that? Surely they could see that it was a scam?"

With dignity and self-esteem stripped away, my "Julia Childs" friend was a lonely middle aged drunk, who painted a cheery façade of a Gourmet Cook to hide her embarrassment.

Faced with the truth in print, I was a lonely (nearly) middle aged drunk who was painting a romantic façade as an exotic Mistress, to hide my humiliation over a tawdry cheap affair with an asshole who had no intention of ever leaving his devastated wife.

The only honest and authentic drunk among us, was Stinky Phil.

Chapter 4. Moderation and the Fuck It Fairy

"A little bit of what you fancy does you good" Lily Boniface, my Grandmother.

You didn't die. At the very least you expected to wake up this morning, unable to move, the left side of your body paralysed, drool dripping onto the pillow. But not even a minor heart attack. That throbbing in your left arm *must mean something*. Maybe you'll die slowly. Maybe your liver, struggling to regenerate, will turn your skin yellow, and slowly poison you from the inside out.

You lie in bed this morning, waiting for the nausea to pass and imagining your demise. You hear your husband grind the beans, the clicking of the gas stove as he heats water. And then, fifteen minutes later, you smell the coffee. Your cue to get up.

You try to assess his mood by the way he clatters around the kitchen. An off key hum, a soft murmuring to the cat, and you can swing your legs out of bed, splash cold water on your face, and ignore the churning in your stomach. Exasperated crashing of pans, followed by the low roar of the dishwasher...well, that could signify a disapproving silence, a blanket of his disappointment over the day.

You can't remember going to bed last night. Again.

You remember leaving work yesterday. You remember the drive home. The Negotiation.

"You don't need wine, you had wine last night"
"*But today was stressful*"
"Just have a cup of tea tonight"
"*But we're having halibut, it's so much nicer with white wine*"
"If you don't have wine tonight, you can have wine tomorrow"
"*But I want it now!*"

Do you remember being self-conscious about going to the same liquor store two days in a row?

The change of route took you to the other side of town, and half an hour out of your way.

"Just tonight then. It's Friday. No point in quitting over the weekend. Monday's better"

Then, once inside the store, there was the second dilemma - one bottle or two?
It's become easier lately, because you've switched to white wine.

One bottle of white wine for you, one bottle of red for your husband.

So now it's win-win, because he never finishes the bottle.

You have to buy a bottle from the cool cabinet, because there's no way you want to wait for the bottle to chill when you get home.

You want to hear the reassuring gasp and sigh as the cork slides out of the bottle, the comforting ritual "glug" of liquid. You want to trace your finger through the slight condensation on your glass. You want to feel the day unhitch from your shoulders, as the alcohol seeps into the neural passages of your brain, pushing away dark and fearful thoughts, and stimulating the pleasure seeking synapses that communicate a comforting whisper.....all is well now....

But first you make feeble conversation with the bored check-out clerk.

"Is this a popular wine? Have you tried it yet?
As if you are some kind of wine journalist doing fucking research.

Then the daily dance when you get home.
Husband: "You bought wine *again*?
You: "Yes, it's been a long day, and it's *Friday*"- defensively, waiting for a negative comment.

Evenings have become predictable. You attempt to ration your *small* bottle, make it last.

Just sip, sip sip.....don't pound it back

In the early days, you could have teased and cajoled for *one more bottle...if you loved me, you would get me another bottle.....*

And he would laugh, and pop out to the liquor store, anything for his carefree *fun* wife.

She loves to party!

You barely feel the buzz from one bottle anymore. You wait, looking at the half –finished bottle of red. The unfinished glass.

How the fuck does he do that? One glass?

But you're glad he does.

It's become a white knuckle ride. You *will* him to go to bed. To leave the bottle. And when he does finally shift and stretch...

"I'll be there in a moment...."

You gulp down a glass. You always intend to pour away the rest, but you never do. You relax into the buzz, just letting thoughts drift and out of your consciousness.

It would be fine if it all just stopped there. But it doesn't, does it? Somehow, a thought will remain wedged in the forefront of your mind, a comment, an imagined slight, and you filter it through different angles, again and again, alcohol blurring the lines of your rationality.

You'll have the vicious text messages to prove it, the incoherent rants on social media. Somehow your brain is able to function on some higher level of consciousness, a wicked corner of yourself that is unleashed only when the rest of you has blacked-out.

Sometimes, in the early hours of the morning, you are tortured by glimpses of this "other you", as you stagger to the bathroom, with the simultaneous urge to pee and gulp down ice cold water.

Every morning you try to shower off the stale reek of wine, but the excess perspiration caused by your liver heating up, attempting to eliminate the poison, means a funk odour constantly hangs around you. Your face is red and flushed, as your skin, the last organ of defence, tries to flush out the toxins.

Your head pounds, your stomach curdles. Only fat, grease and carbs will help your body bounce back from the ever deepening daily plunge in blood sugar – a sure sign of addiction.

You know it has to stop. You know that your marriage is deteriorating. You know that your business is failing. You know that friends have got fed up with your drama and your bullshit.

You know you are killing yourself

Today you must make a change. *Today.*

When I first quit for good, I tried to explain to bemused friends, why I had taken this seemingly punitive action.

"I'm drinking far too much. I need to *stop*"

"Why not just cut down?"

I couldn't cut down because I really loved alcohol. I loved the feeling of looseness, I loved the numbing sensation as it hit the back of my throat, and I loved the warmth as it settled in my stomach. I loved the feeling of reassurance that alcohol gave me.

"Everything is OK now, you've got this"

What I didn't love, of course, were the consequences of drinking.

At 3.00am in the morning, anxiety hit me like the screech of a train entering a tunnel, barrelling towards me.

"Loser, loser, loser"...rattled out the train....

On my sober quest, which started a long time before I actually quit drinking for good, I became intimately acquainted with the "Fuck it Fairy".

For the three or four years, during which it became painfully aware to me, if not everyone around me, who had to put up with my increased level of bullshit and erratic behaviour, I fell into a pattern, that I now refer to as the "Drinking Circle of Doom".

Here's how it works.

I drank – far too much in an evening – let's say Saturday, but in truth, it could have been any day ending in a "y". I fell into bed, after a comatose evening in front of the TV, during which I may have face booked or texted weird and disturbing stuff – as it popped into my mind. I may or may not have started a fight, instigated some drama, or wallowed in self- pity, for some imagined offensive remark, or perceived slight.

All of this is forgotten, until I wake up in the early hours and piece together, in my mind, the evening before. Then I cringe and beat myself up, feeling humiliated and embarrassed and fearful of the damage control that I may have to do. And let's not forget the hangover.

When I finally manage to get on with my day – unproductive, low level hangover, my self- esteem and self-respect down some deep black hole –I promise myself for the millionth time that I won't drink today. I'll have a break. I'll give my liver a rest.

As the day progresses however, and the hangover recedes, and the humiliation of the previous night's behaviour is diluted, a voice starts to whisper in my mind...

Aren't you over-reacting a little? Seriously, no one takes any notice of face book. Really, everyone drinks wine, it's not like you are hitting the 'hard' stuff now is it?

This voice becomes insistent and persistent....until Wine O'clock rolls around, and the Fuck it Fairy steps out of the shadows, and leads you to the liquor store, saying soothing things like "You've had a long day, let's not worry about this silly quitting business now, we'll revisit it on Monday",

And so the Drinking Circle of Doom is set in motion once more.

Sometimes I would revolve around my circle in 24 hours, sometimes a few days, but one thing was certain, the Fuck it Fairy would appear, and any lingering willpower that I had amassed since her last visit would immediately vanish.

The Moderation Debate.

Can anyone "moderate"? Or are we just cast into two categories, an accident of birth or personality defect – either you are an alcoholic or not. Either you can drink "normally" or you are doomed to weekly meetings in dusty Church basements, clutching lukewarm bad coffee. Knowing that you are "just a drink away" from free fall into the dark abyss.

This is a powerful stereotype.

Linked inextricably to this, is the concept of sobriety.

If alcoholics are on the edge of doom, their only salvation is sobriety. Ergo, if you are sober, then you must be an alcoholic.

Completely illogical of course, the same as saying that if all poodles are dogs, then all dogs must be poodles, but being sober in our booze drenched society has *become* so far from normal, most of us automatically assume that if someone is a non-drinker, they must have no choice in the matter.

The stigma. The Shame of being one of the "others".

For a long time, I listened to the insidious message that the Alcohol Industry whispered to me...

'You don't want to be the "other"...a "raving alkie", a weak pathetic person who can't hold your booze. You don't want to be part of that club....keep drinking...you're not like those people"

And so I kept drinking. And attempting to 'control' my drinking.

I hadn't reached Rock Bottom.

I still *looked* OK-ish. I hadn't piled on too much weight.

And I had a solid plan for keeping the weight off – *I saved all my calories for wine! Genius!!*

Like countless other women, I measured the state of my health by the number on the scales. Lower was better.

In my late twenties, I dated an older man, and then stayed with him for fifteen years. He is the reason that I emigrated to Canada.

"You're the fattest girl I've ever been with"...he said to me once, almost in bewilderment. It was true. I had seen pictures of his ex's, and I knew his ex-wife. They were all very thin.

I wasn't huge, but I was certainly a "solid build".

That comment stayed with me, and because I was young and stupid, and he seemed experienced and sophisticated....my mission in life was to transform my solid body, into a sleek, streamlined machine. With muscle definition.

I started running obsessively. This was OK, because Older Man also ran obsessively too. So I entered my miles into a training log, I watched calories (fuel, not food), I measured my waist, thighs and monitored my heart beat and pulse rate.

And I fucking hated every minute.

I even 'competed' in lots of races. Marathons (London, four times,), half marathons and 10k's.

And throughout the entirety of our relationship, Older Man referred to me as "chubby". Not as a description. *As a name.*

Interestingly, when I look back at those fifteen years, although I wasn't drinking to excess (too many calories), I was having to "control" my drinking.

For instance, I would never open a bottle of wine before eight or nine at night (so I would go straight to bed afterwards instead of opening a second bottle – it wasn't a fool-proof method). I would measure the glasses of wine out *exactly, so that I got my exact and equal share....and sometimes I would sneak a gulp out of Older Man's glass if I got the opportunity.*

When the relationship was over, I stopped running and bothering about controlling my drinking.

And here's the bizarre part.........*I got thin!! I dropped about 20 pounds!!*

I existed on Wine and Toast.

The reason I was thin, of course, is that I was stressed and malnourished.

Yet, I was delighted with my skinny appearance. Gone was "chubby girl" and in her place was "Booze-chic girl".

Fast forward a decade or so and the wine calories, paired with greasy carbs to ease the hangovers had made their mark.

 Looking in the mirror, I saw Booze Boobs and a Wine belly.

Added to that, was a puffy red face, dehydrated rough patches of skin and lank hair.

I had stopped really caring about my appearance. Living in a rural suburb of Vancouver Island, the "uniform" consists of blue jeans and a plaid shirt. Conveniently casual and baggy.

And it hid my expanding girth and allowed me to sink into obscurity. I barely looked at myself in the mirror, I avoided cameras and refused invitations that required dressing up. I literally had no other clothes that would fit, and the thought of shopping, and trying on garments under the harsh lights of a fitting room filled me with horror.

So much easier to climb into my PJs earlier and earlier every day, and stagnate with my chardonnay.

I still *functioned.*

It's not as if I'm drunk all day long, I reasoned.

After a disastrous business venture with a partner (which night after night drinking wine did nothing to improve....surprise!), I decided to branch out on my own, and also help out with my husband's business.
I was full of good intentions. Yet, working at home merely opened up more drinking opportunities. Before, I would never had drunk wine at lunchtime - just made up for it when I got home - working from home, I could have a glass or two at lunchtime "just to help me relax and let the creativity flow.". Inevitably, the long lunchtime turned into a snooze on the couch, waking up in time for "wine o'clock" and there "Poof!" Another day gone, and zero productivity from me.

Business meetings and appointments served to shine a spotlight on my loosening grip.......

First, I regularly omitted to *write anything down.*

After some embarrassing incidents when appointments were missed altogether, my husband (not an organizational whizz himself) took to scheduling "reminder calls" the day before the meetings.
This is the way it mostly panned out....

4.00pm. Reminder call about meeting the next day.
4.30pm. I half heartily make a few notes until...
5.00pm I open a bottle of wine.
6.00pm I grumpily go back to making notes....
7.00pm I give up, saying..."I'll get up early and finish prepping for the meeting.
7.01 pm I carry on drinking until I fall into bed...

8.00 am. I wake up feeling groggy and sweaty

8.01am I remember about the meeting...and think "Fuck it, I'll wing it"

8.45am I drag myself out of bed

9.15am I argue with husband about getting ready

9.45 am I am finally out of the shower.

10.00 am. I am dressed, feeling bloated, flushed, sweaty and grumpy...

10.30 am I am in the meeting, trying to focus, while ignoring the pounding behind my left eye.

12.00 noon. Meeting over and we go for lunch.

12.01 pm. I order a large glass of white wine to "celebrate"

I needed a plan.

We went on a diet. Seventeen days of no alcohol, no carbs, no sugar.

I wrote out a menu. I shopped.

We started on a Monday.

Nine days and I was doing well. I had lost a few pounds. I was sleeping better. I had more energy and I was getting stuff done.

Being self-employed is like living constantly on a roller coaster. It's a hard slow grind at first, there are moments of pure exhilaration, followed by a plunge into fear and "what the hell am I doing?"

Sometimes there is a thin line between being *self-employed* and *un-employed,* the former promising a life of Inspiration and Fulfillment....the latter, *twice weekly benefits.*

We were at the fledgling stage of our business. "Start-up" in fact. And times were lean, so my husband in the middle of our new health kick, left for a couple of weeks to work as a contractor at a pulp mill, and I was left with a long "to -do" list to keep the company chugging along.

I would love to write that I made at least 24 hours of not drinking, before

I succumbed. But before Bob had even disembarked from the ferry in Vancouver, I had already had a couple of glasses of wine.

Just today, I told myself, I'll buckle down tomorrow....

Well, tomorrow and tomorrow and tomorrow.......I don't think I had one day free from alcohol *at all*.

I did virtually nothing.

How's the website coming? Bob would ask when he phoned,

"What did you do today?"

I made sure that I was not slurring when I took his call, and lied through my teeth about my daily "accomplishments".

The night before he was due to arrive home, I had VOWED not to drink. But I did.

The alarm went off in the morning,

but I slept through it. I was supposed to pick Bob up from the ferry terminal at 9, and I woke up at 8.35. I stumbled out of bed, hungover, and I managed to stub my toe on the bedpost, and ripped my toenail right off.

The pain speared through the fog, but I wasted precious moments trying to stop the bleeding.

I arrived at the Ferry Terminal (late) unshowered, sweaty, smelling of stale alcohol, with a blood stained wad of toilet paper around my toe.

Bob didn't say a word as he hugged me.

To make ends meet, we took on the odd catering gig.

At the end of a miserable week for me (when I was convinced that I would never be able to kick the booze habit....*it's everywhere, all around me)*, we were booked to cater for a wedding.

It turned out to be a 'red neck' affair - prominent members of the local chapter of the Hells Angels were there, the air was filled with a blue dope haze and I was stuck in a tiny kitchen struggling with vats of mashed potatoes, roast beef and veg, and my husband was outside manning the barbeque.

I was hangover free for once.

I knew from experience that nursing a pounding headache through a twelve hour stint in a kitchen was hellish.

Drunk people from the wedding party wandered in and out of the kitchen and out onto the patio. I was offered a beer, which I took, and I stepped out into the sunshine for a few minutes break.

I watched as one lady lurched into the barbeque and nearly set herself alight with hot chicken grease. My husband grabbed her before she hit the ground, and she began to laugh hysterically.

She was surrounded by several people, who propped her up, and gently led her to the parking lot, where she was bundled into a car, and she left the wedding.

The Bride and Groom hadn't even arrived yet.

I looked at my husband as he cleaned up the barbeque, and picked up stray pieces of chicken.

I couldn't make out his expression. Disgust? Resignation?

 I went back into the kitchen and poured away the beer.

Chapter 5 Wine Bitch

My very first blog post:

"Day Three. Day three is always the wobbly day. Day One is easy, usually because it's Hangover Day – or should I say " Motherfucker of a Hangover Day" rather than the usual " Low level fuzziness which is my daily normal Hangover Day".

Day Three usually follows Day Zero – overdrinking on a scale that means I sleep in an alcohol induced coma on the couch to about three o'clock in the morning – wake up feeling like shit, and then hastily check my phone to make sure I haven't drunk texted, or face booked anything stupid and embarrassing, then fall into bed, to try and get normal sleep, before my husband gets up with the sun.

Then comes Day 1 – aforementioned Motherfucker Hangover Day, and I try and act all breezy and normal, trying to hide the fact that coffee (second in line to my first love, wine) is causing my stomach to do flip flops. If I'm lucky, and I don't have to do any damage control in cyber world, I just spend the day in general misery and self –loathing.

Day 2 – always way better. Coffee tastes good, I usually feel a little smug, the day can be fairly productive (for that read * get a couple of things done*), and I pat myself on the back, because I can, if I really try, make it past wine o'clock without cracking open a chilled bottle of white. Unless of course, my husband pours himself a whiskey, and then I get irrationally pissed that I am missing out, and drive down to the liquor store for the chilled white.

(Note – Somehow – and I am sure I will examine this at some point, I have managed to convince myself that drinking white wine – is not actually drinking….wtf??)

Then comes Day Three. It's always the test. I feel like I have purged and cleansed for two days, and to reward myself, I contaminate my body – YET AGAIN – with a bottle of wine. Or two.

And, dear reader (at this point only me), that has been the pattern for at least ten years. Oh you fucking liar, more like twenty.

Why the change? No, I wasn't checked into hospital, I didn't kill anyone, I just felt like – I am always about a bottle away from achieving my potential – I never get there. I am SO CLOSE to building a truly awesome online business – then I have a couple of glasses of wine, and think, what the hell? I'll write that tomorrow. And tomorrow. And tomorrow.

Tomorrow HAS to be Day Four. No MORE Day Three's"

It was pure FEAR that kept me motivated to stay booze free for the first few weeks after the Red Neck Wedding.

I felt that I had somehow glimpsed 'the Ghost of Jackie's Future".

The irony that it was someone else's embarrassing incident that had scared me dry was not lost on me. After all, I had my own Portfolio of Humiliation that made a drunken episode at a wedding pale into insignificance.

It wasn't just the cringe –worthy moments that played over and over in my mind that were keeping me off the booze. It was the cringe-worthy moments that I had no recollection of *at all* that scared me.

I was scared shitless about the number of blackouts I was having.

Not the " Oh didn't we have a *larf* last night...*what did we do?*" or the kind of woozy memories that come back in embarrassing flashes of you dancing on the table, or doing embarrassing Karaoke, no, I mean the *total loss of memory. FOREVER.*

I still have no recollection of seeing some movies, (although my husband swears that I did) and thank goodness for Netflix, otherwise half of Mad Men wouldn't have made sense, if I didn't have the ability to catch up with episodes in secret (the day after I apparently watched them).

I have no recollection of making phone calls, posting on Facebook, sending emails – only the horror of the evidence the next day, or the confused and irritated texts from friends (and occasionally an ex-boyfriend, I'm ashamed to admit).

I have complete blackouts of conversations and complete situations....*even when it appeared to other people that I wasn't that drunk.*

It was not uncommon for me to have no memory of getting to bed. I woke up at 3.00am, dehydrated, depressed and frantic that I was losing my mind.

I was also frightened that I may have a stroke.

Sometimes, I would lay in the dark, and feel strange sensations in my arms and legs. Occasionally I felt a sharp stabbing pain in my left shoulder. Heart disease? I wondered.

How long before my liver recovers? Do I have permanent brain damage? *How close did I get to killing myself?*

You're not drinking? *My husband asked suspiciously.*

No.

Are you taking a break?

Yes.

Well, that's good.

I wasn't ready to say 'forever'

I was just flirting with sobriety. Trying it on for size. Getting properly acquainted before I made it permanent.

The first challenge to our fledgling relationship came early. I wrote about it.

"I had a lovely productive day yesterday! I cleaned my oven, sorted paperwork, and worked on a proper plan for my business, and felt positive for the first time in a long time.

I took a cup of tea with me to my greenhouse, and re-potted seedlings (a week ago I would have taken wine). I felt a little smug.....*"This isn't so hard....."*

Then, Bam! The evening started to fall apart.

My sister in law turned up for a visit - no problem there, she doesn't drink.

Then, our neighbour turned up with a large glass of whisky for my husband, and a very large vodka for himself.

My husband also hasn't been drinking for the last few days, but I knew the time would come when he would want to drink. Yet, I felt fairly confident that it would be OK, he likes a couple of whiskeys in the evening - I have never liked whiskey (even though I would drink it after all the wine ran out sometimes).

As everyone sat and chatted, I fixated on my husband's drink. I contemplated running out to get wine, so I could enjoy a drink too - I was so mad that I was missing out!

I willed my sister in law to leave, and my neighbour to leave so I could have *a gulp of my husband's whiskey! How messed up is that!"*

I didn't drink.

I went to bed early. I pulled the covers over my head and felt sad and angry.

"Hi I've just found your blog *I can soooo relate to you, day 1 is easy cos you feel like crap but by day 3 you're feeling better and the voice in your head comes with a vengeance. I've done 3 days several times even 5 which was a push!! I've just started a blog too"*

I stared in amazement at my computer screen.

Someone had read my blog. Someone had left a comment.

I checked the stats and nearly fell of my chair.

My blog had been viewed 78 times!

Writing the blog had become an evening ritual.

After I wrote a few paragraphs, I surfed around and found other bloggers. A lady in London "Mummy Was a Secret Drinker". I imagined her voice. I imagined where she lived. *How weird if I actually knew her.*

We all knew each other.

We knew all about the secret drinking. We knew all about the near misses when someone nearly caught us. We knew about hiding our hangovers with bright morning conversations, we knew about the daily "negotiation", we were all part of the same club.

We all had the same FEARS.

I received an email from the mother of a sober blogger that I had communicated with. Not much communication really, I found his blog, posted a comment, and I visited a couple of times, but he hadn't posted for over a month. That's not unusual. Many bloggers stop, for various reasons.

This blogger committed suicide the same day he wrote his last post.

Apart from the grief, his family was grappling with *how to make sense of that.*

I answered the email saying "Drinking and addiction takes you to a dark place, where logic and reason don't apply".

But as I think about this, I know that addiction is only the symptom. Addiction, to alcohol or drugs, or shopping, or the internet, or anything, is our coping mechanism of choice. And once we start to unravel that coping mechanism, as positive as that is, we are in unchartered waters. And this can be our undoing.

I'm ashamed that I am white, middle class, well- educated and in a stable relationship, and I still have a drinking problem"

I feel shame and vulnerability around writing a blog about it, because I feel that I am being "self-absorbed" or "self- promoting"

106

I worry that I haven't suffered enough to be qualified to contribute to the conversation.

But my shame goes further than that. I am ashamed that I didn't live up to my parent's expectations, I am ashamed that I screwed up relationships, or started them in the first place. My list of stuff I feel shame about goes on and on.

A Theodore Roosevelt speech from 1910 says

"It is not the critic who counts; not the man who points out how the strong man stumble, or where the doer of deeds could have done them better. The credit belongs to the man who is actually in the arena, whose face is marred by dust and sweat and blood; who strives valiantly; who errs, who comes short again and again".

By tackling our addiction, we stand on the edge of the arena. By dealing with our shame, without our coping mechanisms, we step into the arena.

A man struggled with his coping mechanism, his addiction, and sadly didn't make it into the arena. My heart breaks for his family.

It would be easy to point to the evil demon alcohol, and blame the loss of this life, as so many others, on an "incurable disease". But if we are truthful with ourselves, this is really only the tip of the iceberg.

Three weeks into my new-found sobriety, FEAR was starting to be replaced by a mew motivator – ACCOUNTABILITY!

My regular posts to my blog "Wine Bitch" was attracting comments and a building readership.

I had cravings most days. But I didn't want to write that I had *failed*. And I didn't want to abandon this new world of camaraderie.

I was also noticing some small improvements:

- My skin looked clearer.

I have always hated my skin. I am very fair (redhead before the grey set in), as a teenager I had dreadful acne, and I've always had very high colour - sort of like I'm blushing the whole time. Years of my skin trying to cope with the daily dehydration of alcohol, and attempting to purge my body of doses of poison, it became dry and itchy, blotchy with large pores that were accentuated by nightly sweating. Now, the blotchiness had subsided. The redness toned down considerably. My pores looked tighter, and the rough dry patches, all but for a couple of areas around my nose, disappeared. For the first time in years, I saw my freckles!

- I was sleeping better.

Apart from feeling refreshed in the morning, the dark circles around my eyes were reduced. I still had days of feeling listless, but in the most part, I felt energetic. My productivity increased, which led to ...

- Less depression.

Getting stuff *done* increased my feelings of *self-worth*. Not having to worry about stupid things I said, or written on face book, having enjoyable evenings with my husband, pottering around in the garden, a cleaner house...a myriad of small things added to my state of general *happiness*.

Chapter 6. The Secret of Sobriety

There is no Big Secret to sobriety. The only way to be sober...is to *not drink*.

The truth is that every drinker loves alcohol. If there were a way that we could quit drinking, without *actually quitting drinking*.....THAT'S the big secret that we all seek.

Unfortunately, this search for a Holy Grail of Sobriety/Not Sobriety can go on for a hell of a long time, before we break down and admit the truth.

And "the truth", as Gloria Steinmen said "Can set you free. But first it will piss you off"

But once you get over being pissed off, you can start actually doing something.

"Doing" rather than "Thinking" was the only way that I got through the first alcohol free weeks.

Yes. Blindly, unquestioningly *doing*. Like a robot, in fact.

The first time I ever felt that I had got my power back *in some small way,* was when I fled into our garden. Unable to stand the noise in my head for one minute more, as I debated jumping in the car to go and get a bottle of wine, for the millionth time, I literally ran into the garden and I stuck my hands in the dirt.

I still feel it. I got dirt under my nails (which I hate) because I didn't wait to look around for gardening gloves (because this would have given me time to change my mind and go and buy wine) and I pulled weeds. Some of them weren't weeds. I cried a bit, and my nose ran, and I couldn't wipe my face to start with, because of the damn dirt, but I kept my hands jammed in there.

And I carried on doing that, the pile of weeds/legitimate plants piling up beside me, with snot and tears on my face.

Gradually, the noise and negotiation in my head lessened to a dull hum.

Action is the key. To start with.

The difference between all the times I had tried and failed to quit drinking and *this time* was action.

I had researched everything I needed to know to quit booze.

I had a 'toolbox" full of sober strategies.

But the first time that my sober tools actually worked.......was the first time that I actually *used them.*

OK, so here are some actions, that may help you feel better, when you are NOT DRINKING....

> 1. *Counting Days. This made me feel, in the early days, that I was making progress. It made me feel, every time that I crossed off another day of sobriety, that I had achieved something. It was a good feeling. Positive. And after I had crossed off a number of days, I would look at my progress, every so often, and especially at*

times when I felt a craving...and I would think, "it would be such a shame to interrupt that perfect pattern of crosses. And so I would grit my teeth, and at the end of the day, cross off another day. And feel grateful. After about 100 days, I found that the other benefits of sobriety were keeping me in gratitude for my sobriety, so I stopped. Just like that. But to start with, for me it helped.

2. *Fake Beer.* I was never a real beer drinker. I was a wine drinker. I tried fake wine and didn't really like most of what I tried, but what I REALLY wanted was to feel like I was getting a treat...I wanted to feel special, when I sat down with a beverage in my hand – I wanted to feel part of grown-up time and I just didn't get that with soda water. Now, looking back, it's bizarre to think that somehow the beverage in my glass should define me (in my mind) as an

adult or not- BUT if I hadn't had THAT issue – I wouldn't have had a drinking problem at all...it wasn't until later on in the sober journey, that I figured this out – but in the early days, I drank fake beer. It also had the added benefit of fooling people at social functions, so I didn't have to deal with the "oh go on, just have one"...problems.

3. *Decluttering and Gardening. Again, early on – I had the familiar problem of what to do when a VERY PERSISTENT craving came on .I knew I had to distract myself somehow...so I started frantically cleaning out closets, and when I had done that, I started gardening. I had to do something with my HANDS to literally stop them opening a bottle of wine. And I heard grandmothers and mother's voice in my head saying...'the devil makes work for idle hands" so I literally kept my hands busy. Now my*

decluttering and the care of my environment, PLUS the creative outlet I found in my garden would later take on a new significance during my sober journey – but again, when I started out I needed an immediate distraction – and you will too. Make it an active project. Make sure you are away from the TV. Whatever it is, it has to occupy your hands and your mind.

4. *Impose a Policy. This is hard one. What I'm talking about here, is an Alcohol Policy for your immediate environment. If you have a partner, or other people in your household that still drink, then part of your policy must be a form of communication/negotiation about your alcohol policy. My policy was this – don't have wine in the house. Gradually, when I was feeling a bit more stable in my sobriety, I was (and still am) Ok with people*

bringing wine into the house for their own consumption – but I didn't and I still do not purchase wine or have it in the house for entertaining purposes.

Now, I know, very well the counter – arguments that are forming in your mind as I speak – firstly, you may have been thinking that you will do this sobriety thing without actually telling anyone. That somehow, you will just casually say, oh, no wine for me today...and hope that no one notices. I get it. You feel awkward and self- conscious at best about this decision – after all, what normal person can't hold their booze? What normal person would make such a drastic decision to give up entirely? Rather than just cut down? And I know that articulating that drastic decision to someone else, even someone you love and trust is akin to admitting that you are a mental case.....a total nut job. But trust me when I say this, telling your loved one that you have struggling with booze probably won't come as a huge shock.

I thought that I had kept my drinking issues under the radar, but my husband was relieved, not shocked when I told him that I wasn't just "taking a break", I was quitting for good.

Secondly, as I am talking about not having wine for entertaining purposes – you may be thinking something along the lines as "well alcohol is everywhere, I can't live in a bubble, I have to be strong enough to resist, I have to get used to this....sure, I agree, you do. But in your own house, you don't have to test yourself. Trust me, there are going to be many tests of your strength along the way. Clear out the booze, and don't buy any. If you partner still drinks, then have them keep their stash somewhere private. If you feel embarrassed about inviting people and not offering wine – for the time being – don't invite them.

The problem is, that when we are looking for the key to sobriety, the big secret we are really looking, in the first instance for a painless convenient gizmo that will magically turn off all desire to drink, but the desire to drink, only goes when we don't drink.

The secret to sobriety therefore is not an action, not a decision, not even a mindset.....it's an inaction. Just don't drink.

Cleaning out the Environment

In Canada, there is a small surcharge on bottles and cans of pop and alcohol (more for alcohol containers for some bizarre reason, after all they are all made of the same material *scratches head in bewilderment *), and it's possible to claim this surcharge back, if you return your empties to a Recycling Depot.

This poses a dilemma for the copious drinkers among us (well, me). On one hand, it's nice to get some money back (almost like you *earned* it), and in the past it was usually enough to buy another bottle of wine (it's only a few cents per bottle, so do the math), BUT on the other hand, there is the shame and embarrassment of the truck load of empties.

"Goodness me"....I would say..."we haven't done our recycling for *ages*" ignoring the exchange of judgmental glances between the Depot staff (imagined).

There was (is) an alternative, we can wait until the local school has a bottle drive to raise money for a sports team, and then the kids (driven by their parents) will come to collect the bottles and cans.

Just before I quit drinking, one of these bottle drives conveniently happened in my neighbourhood.

"Dad, Dad...look at HOW MANY THIS LADY HAS!!!" The kids were whooping with excitement at the goldmine of empties.

My cheeks burned as the "Dad" thanked me, and loaded the clinking bags into the back of his truck.

On Day 42 of sobriety, I had my first taste of freedom.

"I'm taking the recycling to the depot" my husband announced

"I'll come with you"

We cleaned out the back of the truck. I counted out the empty cans.

'Sixty Three" I said to the assistant at the depot.

"They're all pop cans" he said "You only get 5 cents for those"

"Thank you" I beamed, as I pocketed my $3.15.

On Day 100, I wrote a letter to my former self.

Dear Jackie,

You're feeling pretty low at the

moment. *Another day with a hangover. Another unproductive day. Another day despising yourself. You won't believe it right now, because you are too scared and tired, but life is about to change. In 100 days, life will be transformed.*

- *You will acknowledge that you are an Alcoholic. Dysfunctional Drinker. Drunk. Lush. It won't matter what label you use. You will have stopped comparing your drinking to those around you. You will stop telling yourself that 'So and so drinks so much more than me, I must be Ok". You're not. Once you start you can't stop. When was the last time you had just one glass of wine? Never. You have no "Stop Button". But you do have a "Don't Start" button. And over the next 100 days, you will be amazed at how effective that button is. Simple.*

- *You're worried about all those social occasions, where the wine flows freely. What will people say when you refuse wine? What will you say? Will they think you are boring? Will they think you have a problem? News Alert Princess! You do have a problem. Firstly, your health, your work, your whole life is way more important than what a few people think. And here's the thing...you're not that special!!Over the next 100 days, you'll go out as normal, you'll even go camping. And you know what? No one will care if you drink wine or not. Oh, you may have to tell a couple of white lies "Oh, I've given up because I get terrible heartburn", so what? You'll have a fun time, you will chat and laugh as usual.....and you will drive home and remember it all in the morning! Simple!*

- *You'll still going to be in debt in 100 days. The Debt, like all of life's other problems won't magically disappear. But for starters, the $15 per day that you spent on wine will have stopped. So that's $1500 right there. And because you are not wallowing in self-pity and Merlot, you'll remember to transfer money at the right time, and the cash haemorrhage due to NSF charges, and late payment charges will stop. Your business won't have taken off quite yet, but you will be gaining traction, and the quality of your work will have improved. You'll start to feel quite proud of what you do. Simple.*

- *You'll stop beating yourself up about all the fuck-ups you made in the past. All those drunken evenings getting worked up about that toxic relationship, those stupid business mistakes, and the drunken rants on face book? Waking up at 3 am, dehydrated and guilt-ridden, checking your phone, email and social media, to see what you said this time? That will stop. You'll forgive yourself. You'll move on. Simple.*

- *Sorry to disappoint you, but that 30lbs in excess weight that you're carrying? It won't disappear. You've abused your body for over a decade, did you think it would be fixed in 100 days? Get Real. But your skin will be clearer than it's ever been. You'll be sleeping.....yes real refreshing sleep. You will enjoy food. You won't be stressing about one fucking piece of cake, even though you are putting 4200 extra wine calories in your body every fricking week! How crazy is that! Towards the end of the 100 days, you will start to hear what your body is telling you. That it needs a glass of water. Or "tonight I'd like some fresh leafy greens" and because you*

*won't be drowning out that voice with alcohol - you'll
actually listen and act. Your body will thank you by becoming less puffy, and finally the scales will start to move in the right direction. Simple.*

- *You will re-connect with a friend. You're feeling all hurt and annoyed right now. But she was the only one who knew. The only one who called you on your bull shit. She probably saved your life. So you'll finally stop being a whiny princess, and you'll have tea with her. It will be nice. She waited for you to get over yourself. Thank her. It's Simple.*

- *You will start to make a difference. You will write a blog and by Day 100, nearly 10,000 people every month will look at it. Some will leave comments. They will be inspirational and supportive. This blog, and all the other bloggers will keep you*

*going, with words of wisdom,
their own beautiful, uplifting
stories. You will make new
friends. It will be a quiet
revolution, and you will be part
of it. Remember that you used to
want to change the world?
Leave your mark? You will. You
just didn't know how. Now you
do. Simple.*

- *You'll stop looking at your
  husband and wondering if he
  regrets marrying you. He's
  always been supportive and
  loyal. Now you'll be making him
  proud. Simple.*

*Lastly, Jackie, you will start to like
yourself a bit. Oh, you'll still fuck up
on occasion, say the wrong thing,
make the wrong decision. Be all hot-
headed and swear too much. You'll
still procrastinate (can't blame it all on
the vino - sorry!), and you won't be
perfect. But life will be less stressful
and complicated. Guilt will no longer
be your default emotion.*

Simply by putting down the bottle

Love Jackie xx

Giving up alcohol seemed to be such an overwhelming concept, that every time I even thought about it, I just argued that thought right out of my mind.

"Don't be silly, I thought, 'everyone drinks alcohol it's fun – you are over reacting!"

And I would carry on with my foolish and doomed attempts to moderate – to just drink on weekends – but weekends include Fridays – that's the start of the weekend, and Wednesday is hump day, so just a small drink then, and if I drank on Wednesday and I'm going to drink on Friday, I might as well drink on Thursday too .....I'll just get this weekend over with, and I'll start on Monday...It went on and on.

Moderation seemed a logical response to the problem, quitting booze completely not only seemed like taking a sledge hammer to a nut – it also seemed like a huge unobtainable goal with uncomfortable consequences for all areas of my life.

Big Goals are LIKE that. No one ever run a marathon without the physical discomfort of training, no one ever wrote a novel without shutting themselves away for hours, thumping away on typewriter – NOTHING worth achieving is EASY or without discomfort.

But quitting drinking is far more than exercising discipline – it means undertaking some honest reflection on your life, taking stock of WHY we are where we are, and moving out of our comfortable sphere into the vast unknown.

When I really began to drink heavily, I had one more failed relationship and a fading career in real estate. I had always felt like I hadn't really lived up to my potential for a career and relationships never seemed to work out, but my response always had been to run away – jump into another relationship right away, try another career, without really figuring out what went wrong. Instead of doing the hard work of learning some lessons, I blotted it all out with wine.

I've always been a procrastinator. I've always taken the easy road, and the popular road, YES has always been the easiest word to say, I struggled with NO, because maybe people wouldn't like me? And then, once I had said YES, I resented it....how often did I do this, agree to do something I really didn't want to do, then get all resentful, and do it with bad grace?

And all of these bad feelings, and overwhelm from put off tasks, small things that built into mammoth stressors, and I ran to the bottle to numb all these feelings that I didn't want to feel.

So, in a sense the first phase of sobriety was the simplest – focusing on the strategies, distracting myself when the Wine Witch came to visit – it wasn't EASY, but it was straight forward.

The next phase was hard – the growth phase.

I had to grow into the type of person who doesn't procrastinate over the small stuff. I had to grow into the type of person who deals with small issues head on, and gets them out the way before they overwhelm me.

I had to grow into the person who can say NO. Who can protect my boundaries. And also become the person who says YES, after thoughtful consideration – and then OWNS the decision, and carries it out with good grace.

I had to grow into the person who can sit with emotions – even sadness and anger and experience them – because that's part of being a human being.

When I talk about BIG GOALS, I don't necessarily mean achieving success in the sense that I become a CEO of a vast company, or write a best seller, although these thing are far more possible in sobriety, my goal was to live life without a chemical crutch, without an artificial prop, without a substance that rounds off all the edges.

I read a passage in Anne Lamott's book "Travelling Mercies' recently, where she describes the demeanour and attitude of a friend who had cancer in its last stages, and she wrote

"He's so savouring the moments of his life right now, so acutely aware of love and small pleasures that he no longer feels that he has a life threatening disease: he now says he's leading a disease – threatening life"

So how do you lead a disease-threatening life?

Respect Your Body.

We only get the one body. And, let's face it, most of us don't make our health our first, second or even third priority. We're too busy to exercise properly, we (in the Western World) eat far too much, but are severely malnourished, most of us are chronically dehydrated, we smear ourselves with scented cancer inducing chemicals, and yes, for decades we slowly poison ourselves with booze. And then we expect our over stretched health care systems to "cure" our cancers, our diabetes, our heart disease and whatever other chronic conditions that would be completely avoidable if we had only respected our body in the first place.

I heard a sad story about a lady who had drunk so much over the years that her liver failed. Every Friday she is wheeled into the hospital for her body to be drained of all the fluid that has built up. But, she still expects to be "cured", as does her husband - who cannot conceive that the health professionals simply cannot do anymore for her. They cannot grasp the fact that she is very near death. And it could have been avoided.

Imagine how that would feel. Imagine being told that you will never see your children grow up, you will never see grandchildren, you will never enjoy your golden years......all because you carried on disrespecting your body.

It still terrifies me - did I stop soon enough? Did I do any damage? Is that twinge in my arm a sign of an impending stroke? How irresponsible, how stupid!! I beat myself up and then I remember that not only should I respect my body, it's also essential to

Respect My Soul

We are filled with anxieties, with stress, we lie awake ticking off our failures in our minds.....it starts in schools, where we are "taught" in rigid systems that don't inspire or encourage creativity; our society penalizes the inventive child who can 'see' diverse solutions to problems, but cannot spell; we are conditioned at an early age to measure our worth against a set of standardized tests, that map out our path before our brains and minds are fully developed into their unique splendor.

As adults, the sum of our successes are measured in four door sedans, annual all- inclusive vacations, and granite counter tops.

We are spiritually barren, unless you count a weekly session of "hot" yoga, and the new Anthony Robbins Infomercial on Netflix.

When did we last spend a day by the ocean, just marveling at the power and beauty of Mother Nature? When did we last just nurture a garden, get lost in the moment, with our hands in the dirt, to which we will eventually return - and contemplate Love, Joy, Gratitude, and our real place in the universe?

Or, did we just crack open another bottle of Merlot, and catch up with Batchelorette?

Respecting Dreams

Remember when you first picked up a camera, took a picture, and someone

told you "Wow, you have a good eye!"
Or you worked for weeks at the
outline of a novel, or fussed over a
*new design for that invention? But
then put it down - because..."I don't
have time"..."I don't have the
cash"......"I might fail"*

*Or maybe you procrastinated, like I
did. Always intending to "start next
week"....but it was always, always,
easier to pour another glass, and
pontificate about another grandiose
scheme. And then do nothing.*

*Drinking is the antithesis of Self Care
and Self Respect.*

*Joan Didion once wrote of self-
respect-*

*"There lies the great, the singular
power of self- respect. Without it, one
eventually discovers the final turn of
the screw: one runs away to find
oneself, and finds no one at home."*

I had one hundred days of sobriety. I
was on my way home, but I wasn't
there yet.

Chapter 7. Keith Richards, Crab Traps and Feminists

Dear Jackie,

This is an email that I've written a thousand times in my mind. Maybe I should have send it sooner. But I've distanced myself because so often you've send me strange texts, or emails, which were obviously written while you were drunk, and in the morning you don't seem to remember them......I miss the friendship we had.....

C.

The hardest part of putting down the bottle, I found, was surveying the wreckage afterwards. The wreckage, which I myself had created. And then, DO something about it.

Firstly, I had to eliminate the Drunken Drama in my life.

Let me be clear what I mean when I say "Drama". After all we all think we know what it is, but it's a bit like Jazz for some people – we don't know exactly how to define it, but we know what it is when we hear it.

"Drama" I define as a situation or incident that could be very easily resolved by two or more people communicating calmly and reaching a consensus of opinion, or at least an understanding of each other's point of view, but instead, is escalated into a negative angry conflict, devoid of any reasonable communication, usually with one or more parties determined to play the role of victim.

Drama, as I have defined it, is energy draining, negative, time consuming, tiresome, and if taken to the extreme, damaging to your relationships and in some cases, your health.

So why do we participate? Or even instigate drama?

Well, for me, most of my drama originated when I was drinking, of course...and really involved me in a starring role as victim of some perceived wrong doing, or something that I felt should have been done or said, but wasn't.....ALL completely in my own mind. And in hindsight, my impulse to play the victim, came from the fact that I didn't like myself, I hated what I was doing, and creating drama, with me as the persecuted one, in some twisted way, rationalized my behaviour. Gave me a reason to drink.

After all, if people are so mean to me, I have to drink right?

People got very tired of my drama. They were fed up of my self-pitying posts on face book, my drunk texts, my self- righteous emails, and most reasonable people, like my friend C drifted away from me.

So, when I quit drinking the first behavioural modification was to address the drama. And the first way to do that was to start communicating clearly. And this meant working on my boundaries.

For instance, when someone asked me for something, instead of saying YES, when I wanted to say NO, and then bitching away, (probably to someone else) about the thoughtlessness of this poor person who should have the temerity to request something of me, clearly not CARING how busy I was...thus making myself both a victim AND a Martyr in my Drama Scene.....I said NO. No drama, no victim, proper adult communication.

The first step to eliminating drama in my life, was to eliminate my own.

The second step is to eliminate everyone else's....the drama that you are sucked into, that intrudes into your life, and takes precious time away from you leading the best, most inspiration creative sober life you possibly can and this is a little harder.

Communication is one key, as I have mentioned. Also, identifying the Drama Creators is essential.

Luckily, as soon as it becomes apparent that you have become a *non- drinker* – The Dramatists in your life are sure to reveal themselves.

The Big Adjustment.

When we make a big lifestyle change, it's not only tough for us, it can be a bit unsettling for everyone around us. And it can take a while for people to adjust to the new sober you. While you are trying on your new sober life for size, and getting comfortable – everyone else is getting used to seeing you in this brand new outfit.

Sometimes the reactions that you get, aren't always as positive and supportive as you might hope.

Especially upsetting can be a negative reaction from your close family.

As shocked as you might be – this is actually quite normal. In families, or small close knit communities, we often take on a role. For example, your brother (like mine) might be the sensible one, the person who helps everyone through their financial problems, or your Mum might be the peace maker – getting everyone to get along, and put their differences aside. I didn't know, it, and I definitely didn't intend it – but I was the "problem child" – with two divorces behind me, plus financial mayhem, no real clear career path – the rest of my family had got used to picking up the pieces behind me – they expected disaster and crisis.

So when I made this change, I started to be more confident, it was unsettling for everyone that, for once, I didn't need rescuing. And for a while they didn't really believe it – and frankly, they were a bit skeptical at first.

But eventually, they got used to it. And my role has changed. I'm not sure what it is yet- but I know it's not the role of problem child any more.

Other people in your life, might not adjust with ease.

For comparison purposes, I have divided up the reactions that you may encounter into several categories. I myself have experienced all of them.

"NORMAL" DRINKERS.

These are people that you know slightly, that previously you used to ignore. This is because when you used to offer them wine in the afternoon (to legitimize your own drinking) they used to say things like

"Wine? Gosh, what are we celebrating?" or
"Wine? No thanks, just tea for me"

They also used to do strange things like not finishing a glass of wine. Leaving a half-finished bottle of wine on the table. Spend their weekends doing "non-drinking activities" like hiking, or outdoor sports, or anything tended that compromise your drinking time...so you didn't take part, even when invited.

In short, these people CONFUSED THE CRAP out of you.

Shortly after I gave up drinking, Bob and I went camping for the weekend.

I didn't want to go.

I prepared by packing lots of non-alcoholic beverages. I included fake wine, because it at least looked like booze, and therefore, I reasoned, people would be less likely to realize that I wasn't drinking.

I needn't have been concerned.

No one cared about the beverage in my glass. I was worrying for nothing.

It was exactly like the time when I was twelve and whining to my mum about having to change into my swimming costume on the beach. I attempted to hold a towel round me, and clamber out of my underwear and pull on my costume *with one hand.*

Hold the towel for me, I whined.

For God's sake, my mum said in exasperation....

No One is LOOKING AT YOU............

SUPPORTIVE FRIENDS

These friends are those true friends that you abandoned because of their annoying habit of Calling You On Your Bullshit.

Yes, the friends that used to say "I'm getting a bit worried about you, you texted me last night, were you drunk again?"

You ditched them, because they were FUNBUSTERS (or so you told yourself) and gradually they disappeared from your life, because you were rude, obnoxious, and self-absorbed.

I wrote back to my friend C.

Dear C,

I'm glad you wrote that email. It's very hard for me to write this down, but I know that I have a problem with alcohol....

These days, C and I meet for tea. It isn't the same as the evening we used to spend, putting the world (and our boyfriends) to rights, with a couple of bottles of wine.

It's different. It's better.

DRUNKEN IDIOTS_

These people are basically annoying but harmless. They drink copious amounts, and say stuff to you like "Oh shit, are you still on the wagon?" But basically they don't care if you drink or don't drink. Because they are too drunk to give a crap.

But don't write them off. Take a good look.

I've met myself many times at parties.

I can see myself clearly.

I'm the one surveying the bar to see how much booze is available.

I'm the one sneaking a top-up from the box of wine, rather than the bottle, because no one can see how much I've drunk.

I'm the one standing, a little unsteadily, but focusing VERY HARD on the conversation.

I'm the one, talking a little too loudly, laughing too loudly and repeating myself.

I'm the one, who people refer to when they wake up with a hangover the next morning...

"Geez, how much did I drink last night? Hope I didn't say anything too embarrassing. Oh well, at least I didn't drink as much as Jackie!"

PEOPLE SUFFERING FROM "KEITH RICHARDS" SYNDROME.

I love Keith Richards. The (now elderly) Rolling Stones Guitarist who has survived drug, alcohol, and nicotine addiction on an unprecedented scale, yet is still performing to sold out world-wide rock stadiums is often touted as the Proof that all the Health Professionals are Wrong.

Or, if not Keith Richards, it's amazing to me how many people have an elderly aunt, who has thrived into her nineties, while existing HER WHOLE LIFE solely on a bottle of wine a day, LARD and cigars.

Look at the internet if you need further examples.

Check out the research that suggests that three glasses of champagne a day will keep Dementia away, or a glass of red wine is 'equivalent" to working out at the gym for an hour.

People may mock your sobriety.

"You won't live longer if you quit drinking, it will just feel like it"

"We've all got to die of something!"

"If I die from drinking, at least it will have been fun!"

Actually, some of these comments have a grain of truth.

Many people take a long time to die from alcohol abuse. There are several stages, that include cognitive

impairment and brain shrinkage,
stroke or heart problems, diabetes
and of course liver and kidney failure.

But even in the last stages, when
internal organs shut down, and the
body is unable to eliminate fluid,
medical science can keep you alive for
years. But you will have to visit the
hospital once a week, so a kind nurse
can shove a large needle in your
stomach, and literally drain out all
the liquid that has caused your
stomach to distend like a hideous
balloon.

So yes, we all have to die of
something. But that way doesn't
sound like *fun.*

FEMINISTS

My ability to 'drink the boys under
the table" was always a badge of
honour for me.

So I get it, when I hear rumblings
from women along the lines of ....

'Men have had all the fun time in the pub over the years, it's our time now"

"Men have a beer after football, why shouldn't we have wine at the book club?"

Times, they are a'changing.

My mum has never set foot in a Bar on her own. I not even sure if she has ever purchased alcohol on her own. She would never drink alone, and while us kids were at home, I never remember her having a "girls night out".

Times are different now and that's better. There shouldn't be places where it's 'taboo' for women to frequent, and we all need relaxation time.

But the big problem is that feminism has been warped and twisted into a *marketing pitch.*

And more disturbing, it's not only feminism that has been used by the Marketing Industry to sell booze, it's also Motherhood.

OK, disclaimer: I am not a mummy. Unless you count three beautiful unique stepkids, two in their 30's and one in her late twenties. So I am not familiar with the raising of children from the small squirmy poo machines, through the sullen teens and out the other side as wonderfully balanced, fully fledged accomplished humans. Ha.

But, I do not regret NOT having children (I know, so *unnatural and selfish*), because I have observed you all doing the parenting thing and I can see that, as much as you deny it, it's not as sparkly and unicorny as you thought when little Jimmy was just a horny glimmer in Daddy's eye.

It's not always fun. I get it. As one of my friends said, as she washed poo out of her hair, and wiped out the mustard coloured content of a diaper off the floor (toddler tantrum)

"I didn't think it would be as hard as this"

The problem is, according to the Mummy Propaganda, it's not supposed to be hard, it's supposed to be full of joy. AND, you are supposed to be an expert. Immediately. AND you are supposed to still be independent, career savvy, calm, organised, and a good housekeeper (even if you weren't before the baby was born). You're supposed to be able to pick the good school, and remember to register, engage your child in "developmental" activities, before they can even sit upright, breast feed until the kid is (insert correct age according to most recent research), make your own organic solid baby food....the list is long and expectations are high.

No wonder you guys are all hitting the bottle. Luckily for you, the Alcohol Industry is there to make your lives all better.......and if we are to believe all the social media hype, it would appear that not only does the Merlot make you Mellower, Hip Parents, it also smooths out all the rough edges of soccer practices, music recitals and toddler birthday parties...

First of all, from the safety aspect, what if the kids are sick in the middle of the night and you need to rush them to the hospital?

And from a logistics and planning point of view, I can't imagine being woken at five in the morning by a toddler demanding attention, or dealing with the school run, or facing the minefields of Lego, playdough and the *really irritating toys that speak,* with a pounding hangover...

I'm all for choices, and women having the right to make all those choices that affect our lives - whether to have children or not, whether to be a working parent or not, to have equal pay, to be respected for the job of motherhood - THE most important task for humankind - to have access to proper childcare, women's health facilities, the list goes on and on, and we need to exert our power in the democracy in which we live, and never back down.

But wine drinking? C'mon...seriously?

Do you think that suffragettes, when they chained themselves to railings, really envisioned their legacy as women having the *right* to slurp chardonnay on the couch every night?

We're being conned.

The Alcohol Industry is dominated by men. They are targeting women. Up until the 1990's we didn't really "perform" well when it came to our consumption of booze. Now, with careful, targeted marketing - yes, products packaged with catchy names like "Mummy Juice", "Bitch", "Skinny Girl"......we are now closing the gender gap in alcohol consumption with men. Although statistics are sketchy, mainly because the research relies on self-reporting, and hell, who tells the truth about that?, the stats on female driving while impaired, women admitted to hospital with alcohol related medical emergencies, women with liver disease (some in their thirties!) has risen exponentially in the last decade.

It seems that men can exert control over women's lives in many ways.........

But when we stumble drunkenly, we stumble *hard*.

There's nothing that society vilifies and hates more than a Bad Mother.

The media shows no mercy to women who are caught drunk while in charge of children.

Don't get me wrong, I'm not condoning for one second, the behaviour of any woman or man who puts the lives of children at risk.

I am merely pointing out the hypocrisy of it all.

Where are the "sistas" who post memes about the "winebulance" when a mum is picked up with a DUI?

Where are all the 'feminists" who say "go on, just one more won't hurt" knowing that you'll have to drive home from your book club meeting?

Where are all the giggling soccer mums, passing round the hip flask of vodka at Saturday morning kids practice, when one of their gang turns up in Court?

SABOTEURS AND THE CRAB TRAP SYNDROME

Saboteurs are stealthy. They come disguised as friends. At first they will feign concern

"Oh poor you, do you really have to give up FOR GOOD?"

They will try to test you.

"Oh go on, just one won't hurt"
Then they will openly try to sabotage you.

"Oh, you won't last....remember when you tried to give up chocolate, that only lasted a week, just have a drink

for God's sake, don't be so fucking uptight, have some fun...."

These people have some power, IF YOU LET THEM....because they are often family members or people you regarded as friends. So it's hurtful.

These people are behaving like crabs in a crab trap.

No one really knows why, (or maybe no one has been able to tell me so far) but it is a marine FACT, that crabs, once they've wandered into a trap, will prevent each other, by clawing them back, from leaving the trap – even though there is an easy unobstructed exit route available.

In the same way, some people will try and hold you back, even though the same inspirational path to growth is available to them.

After all, EVERYONE can quit booze right?

Yes, but it's hard. It sounds simple, but clawing your way out of the trap takes some tenacity and determination. And along the way, you will develop *character and integrity*.

"Integrity" is one of those buzz words that we tend to over-use when we are writing our resumé .We list it down, in such sentences as...

"My greatest strengths are determination, attention to detail and integrity".

But here are the definitions:

"The quality of being honest and having strong moral principles; moral uprightness." OR

"Having *integrity* means doing the right thing in a reliable way. It's a personality trait that we admire, since it means a person has a moral compass that doesn't waver"

I can tell you that my integrity, during my drinking era became quite bruised and battered.

I was never honest when I was drinking.

I lied about how much I was drinking, I told a myriad of lies to cover up my drinking. When I look back, there are many moments when I can tell you that I didn't act in accordance with the *lowest* standards of moral uprightness. And even though I knew what I was doing was *wrong,* I kept on doing it anyway, and just spent a lot of mental energy, *rationalizing it all to myself.*

I also spent a great deal of time trying to be what other people wanted (or that I *thought* they wanted).

That, of course, caused me a lot of anxiety and stress. (Which I immediately numbed with booze). A Vicious Circle.

As soon as I started to live life according to my values, two things happened.

1. A lot of people got really pissed off

2. My stress and anxiety started to reduce.

Chapter 8 Best Ideas

In the 1970's, my favourite TV show was called "The Good Life".

For those of you who did not have access to the BBC, or are not as old as I am (and probably don't remember the 'Really Hot Summer of 1976", or the Queen's Silver Jubilee *either*), this classic sitcom was about a couple who decide to become "self-sustaining" and live off the grid. Except that they did this in one of the posh suburbs of London, much to the horror of their upper-middle class neighbours. The comedy was the interaction between the neighbours, as the first pig was introduced to the back garden, and the front lawn is ploughed up for the potato patch, and so on.

I just thought it was really cool. That you could actually DO that. (I hadn't clued in that it was a *sitcom*). And it was always my dream (and I have pursued it in many different ways over the years) to live a life that is *far more simple.*

Don't get me wrong, I love technology, and advances in science, and new inventions. In fact my husband is an inventor.

I have just always really wanted to do two things – grow my own food and write my own books.

But life gets remarkably complicated. Before you even realize it.

Firstly – parents, once they have invested into your education, not surprisingly, have loftier ambitions for you, than weeding the garden daily.

Secondly – you are told that happiness won't come from the short stories you have lovingly crafted, or carrots.

Thirdly – you need actual money to live on, which doesn't come from the short stories you have lovingly crafted, or carrots.

Fourthly – you often meet other people who tell you that accounting is far more exciting than it sounds (it isn't. Not for me anyway), and persuade you to leave the short stories and carrots in a drawer. (metaphorically – no carrots were actually left in drawers)

So I abandoned the dreams of my seven year old self, and became an accountant, and married a perfectly nice man, and both of those things didn't last.

After many years of lots of other things and people not lasting in my life – and a growing realization that time on this planet is short, and I had already mis-used a fair proportion of my allocation – I started to drink. Because then I wouldn't have to think about it. And handily for me, for once I seemed in sync with lots of other people who had also abandoned the dreams of their seven -year-old selves, and had maybe divorced, or were weighed down with debt and jobs they didn't like, and had similarly become all disillusioned – because they were drinking also.

So, for a while, it all seemed as though this would be the way it was *supposed* to be.

Except that it wasn't. And it isn't. *Hence this book.*

In a strange way, life has come full circle.

After I put down the bottle, and quit the job (it really quit me), and started to plough up the front garden, and write stuff again, I found out that I will probably never be rich, because money doesn't come from short stories and carrots – but at least I am finally pursuing my dream.

And it turns out that I am a lot more creative than I thought!

But I haven't got a single creative bone in my body

At least, that's what I used to tell myself. And believe.

"I'm not creative, I'm a numbers person. A science person. I don't waste my time with fanciful notions of creativity – I put away those childish things – literature, poetry, dance, art, inventions........you name it, I'm not good at it, and if I'm not good at it, what's the point of doing it?"

What a sad state of affairs. Yet, I'm betting that I'm not the only one who is carrying around these limiting beliefs about my capacity to create – and I bet those beliefs don't have any basis in reality.

It's so often that we think we can only focus on activities in our life that lead ultimately to *achievement.* We put such great emphasis on "success". And we abandon all those things that we just do...because we like doing them.

Here's s another fallacy that I clung on to rationalize my drinking......*it will make me more creative!*

A kind of "Boozey Muse"

Ernest Hemingway, a famous Drunk and Author is quoted often as saying "Write Drunk and Edit Sober"

He never actually said this, and according to his daughter, NEVER wrote while he was drunk. Apparently, he rose early, wrote in a disciplined fashion for hours every morning, and then headed off to get shitfaced in the afternoon.

Of course, if you drink lots (like I used to) and always wanted to be creative (like I do), then the tendency is to cling on to the "Tortured Addict Artist" stereotype, as it serves you well.

And if you don't identify with Ernest Hemingway, there's a whole bunch to choose from... Hunter S Thompson, Dorothy Parker, Raymond Chandler, Dylan Thomas, Truman Capote.... the list of revered drunkard writers is seemingly endless......*who must have created their best work under the influence....surely?*

Fascinated with writer's lives, I would scan biographies to find any snippet of information that I could identify with, rather than get on with the arduous process of actually writing.

And every time I found a reference to drinking, well, that just reinforced my notion that the quantity of booze that I consumed was directly correlated to how creative I could be.

It's as ridiculous as saying "I drive much better after I've had a few......"

When I drank lots of wine, I truly believed (regularly) that I stumbled on the plot of a bestseller, invented ingenious products, and had grandiose business schemes........all fading away - if I even remembered them - in the wake of next morning's hangover.

Drinking is the opposite of creativity.

Drinking dulls the mind, atrophies the brain, diminishes our energy, and sucks away our motivation. Think about the 'activities" that you used to do while drinking. If you were anything like me, you had a MILLION fabulously creative ideas half way down a bottle of Merlot – which evaporated into thin air before you reached the bottom on the bottle.

It's not for nothing that we have the saying – Genius is 10% inspiration and 90 % perspiration – that's what creativity is....and we can only focus and perspire and stick with these amazing ideas, if we are sober.

So here's the other aspect of creativity – it's not just the expansion of our abilities, and pushing the boundaries of what we perceive are our limits – it's the PROCESS of creating that really protects our sobriety.

I remember summers, as a child which were entirely devoted to building Go- karts for example – and myself and a group of my friends would devote hours and hours to fixing them, or making them go faster, or re-building them after crashes – and we would be SO engrossed in these projects that all our parents would be completely exasperated because we would always be late in to dinner.

Well, that all sounds really nostalgic, but scientists have since discovered, that being within that "flow and focus" of creating is what TRULY makes us happy and content.

Psychologists have discovered that it's not the END result that causes the greatest happiness, it's the process.

A long time ago, after I had left education, and was working in a soul-sucking job for a property development company based in Weybridge, I started studying Psychology via the Open University just for the hell of it. (Actually, I had to do something to stop my brain from atrophying).

I really enjoyed the course, and one of the texts that we had to read, stayed with me.
Mihaly Csikszentmihalyi, a prominent social psychologist, researched

happiness.* He found (along with many other researchers) that after a certain level of material well- being has been reached, no further increase in material wealth will increase our level of happiness. Or motivation.

His research, firstly with creative people such as artists and musicians, and then further research with factory workers, found that we are most happy when we reach a "flow" state.

Very simply, a flow state is when you are so absorbed in your activity that you don't notice the time, you don't realize that you have missed a meal....you are totally and utterly *in the zone...*

And this state could be achieved, even if the work, on the face of it, is mundane and repetitive.

I saw this phenomena for myself during a weekend to Quadra Island, which is a small Gulf Island off the East Coast of Vancouver Island. We stayed in a Lodge which had no TV sets and limited wi-fi. But instead, it had glorious views of the ocean and access to rugged West Coast beaches.

We were there for a wedding, so the Lodge was full of family, and although that sounds busy, and potentially ripe for drama, somehow the peace and tranquility got to everybody.

I spent a whole day with my sister-in-law Debra, just poking and prodding around the beach, turning up pretty pebbles and shells, and marveling at beautiful pieces of driftwood.

Debra is one of the most creative people I know. As I have always considered myself rather lacking in the Creativity department, I always hope that Debra's gift will magically rub off on me.

Debra studied Art for about 6 months at a college on the Island, but never graduated – she said that there were too many rules, she had learned what she needed to know, and she couldn't care less about certificates and diplomas. Throughout her life, she has never let lack of knowledge or experience stop her from trying new things. (For instance, that particular weekend she was trying out wood burning techniques with a weird looking branding iron, and was looking for suitable bits of driftwood to practice on). She also passes on EVERYTHING she learns to anybody who asks. She is unfailingly generous with her help and advice.

For a career she is an Educational Assistant, working with some of the most deprived and dysfunctional children in our community. She does two things – she feeds them -usually with cash out of her own pocket, and by asking local businesses to help – she just presents herself at their offices, asks for help, (if you don't ask, you don't get, is her motto) and when they inevitably cannot refuse her – she rewards them with massive

Thank You cards – the results of the second thing she does with the kids – involve them in Art projects. Carving, painting, you name it, she does it with the kids. She trusts them with knives, scissors, carving instruments (and most recently, hot branding irons) and disregards all "school policies" that try to confine her activities to those that they consider "safe". She has never had a child that has hurt themselves. She has many badly behaved children who have never had proper guidance from parents who suffer from all kinds of addictions, and are very often victims of abusive childhoods themselves. The kids behave with Debra. She insists on respect for her and everyone else in the class. The kid comply, because they don't want to miss out on any project that Debra has in mind.

I asked Debra if she was trying to 'save' the kids.

She was confused. "i can't save anyone. All I do is make sure they have fun"

I asked her about addiction. She said this.

"If you are having fun, and loving what you do, why would you pick up a drink?"

I asked her about my own (lack of) creativity, and whether I could learn....

"you're making it too complicated. You just think of something that you'd like to create and then figure out how to make it. But it has to be fun, otherwise why bother?"

Once my wine fog lifted, and I found myself with far more time on my hands that initially I had to FILL with ANYTHING and FAST I got *curious.*

I tried gardening, I started writing my blog, I even got my sewing machine out again.

As Elizabeth Gilbert says in her book "Big Magic" – "Curiosity is the secret.

Curiosity is the truth and the way of creative living. Curiosity is the alpha and the omega, the beginning and the end. Furthermore, curiosity is accessible to everyone"

Happiness v Pleasure

Everyone who has slumped down into the couch after a long day, and taken a swig of chilled chardonnay, can tell you what pleasure is.........or has scoffed a large bowl of Rocky Road ice cream....it's that moment of euphoria, where you slip momentarily away from your trouble into a pleasurable state. BUT, as we know, that moment is usually short-lived.

Who remembers that the second glass of wine was never quite as satisfying as the first? I do. We never quite capture that initial sensation of pleasure.

And that right there, is the very definition of addiction, chasing after something that is just out of your grasp, again and again.

One of the worst habits that we have to break – apart from obviously the actual drinking – is this constant need for instant gratification.

We live in a world that basically relies on instant gratification. We have instant entertainment, instant information, fast food, instant connection, and therefore our values and our sense of wellbeing have got well, *skewed*....

We are mistaking PLEASURE for HAPPINESS....

We want shortcuts to feel good. And that is (I believe) just as hard an addiction to break, as the actual physical, chemical dependency that we have on alcohol.

This isn't new. Human beings have been looking for the quick fix of instant pleasure and the problem as I see it, is that we confuse this with our quest for happiness.

Our overall goal as human beings is to seek happiness. This isn't just a tag line for beauty pageant contestants – it's a recognized purpose of human life, from as far back as Aristotle – and if we needed any further endorsement – we can look to the American Declaration of Independence that lists the pursuit of happiness right up there with liberty and life itself.

But, anything worth having, it worth working for.

First of all, we get this happiness thing all the wrong way round. We think that if we have the RIGHT job, we are the RIGHT weight, we get the RIGHT partner – then and only then will we be happy.

OR, we think that happiness should be somehow "provided" to us by the other people in our lives.

Happiness is something that we create ourselves. And that takes some work and some time – rather than the quick fixes that we have been used to.

Psychologists have done experiments with kids – offering them ONE chocolate bar right now...OR if they are prepared to wait....THREE chocolate bars in a few hours.

Children overwhelmingly choose the ONE chocolate bar NOW.

This is very much like the "drinkers" response to pleasure. We want it now. We want the instant gratification of that glass of wine.

Someone in my life recently described alcohol dependency as "immature" and we should "grow up". Although this sounds a little callous, I do understand what they meant

The mature adult attitude towards happiness should be along the lines of 'If it is to be, it is up to me"

In the same way that we as drinkers yearn for the quick fix, we shy away from the opposite feeling of unhappiness.

We hate those uncomfortable, inconvenient sad moments. We loathe feeling low, and all scratchy in our own skin. We want to fix that RIGHT NOW.

When I first lived on my own, I hated it. I loathed being by myself. Being responsible – not only for all the practical things in my life – but also being completely responsible for my own emotions. There was no one else around me to blame for my sadness or my loneliness, and no one to complain to either! So I made friends with wine. And together we sulked away evenings.

But clearly I wasn't any happier. And I wasn't any likely to GET any happier any time soon, and I imagine that for the few number of brave souls who took the time to care about me – I wasn't a lot of fun to be with.

It wasn't until I took responsibility for CREATING my own happiness that things started to get better. And it didn't just instantly get better just by putting down the bottle either. Please don't get the idea that happiness will miraculously "appear" once you take away the booze. It's a great start – but there's more work to do.

And that's when Gratitude is the key…

I know. *Gratitude,*

You can't scroll down your face book news feed without seeing a post from some self-help guru spouting off about *gratitude.*

Annoyingly, they are right.

And here's the science:

All those little pleasure synapses in our brains that have relied on the daily dose of booze to get them all fired up, have to learn how to do that *all on their own. Otherwise, we would all be pretty miserable for the rest of our life.*

To help the brain with this healing activity, we can work out the little pleasure synapses, by consciously focusing *on stuff that make us smile. Stuff that makes us feel grateful.*

It doesn't have to be the Big Stuff. It can be the daily things that we often take for granted. The feel of clean sheets on your skin. The smell of fresh brewed coffee in the morning. The warmth of your cat resting on your lap.

As my journey progressed, I knew that I had to find some good stuff to fill the Wine Shaped Hole in my life. I just didn't think that spending the rest of my life "in recovery" was going to do the job.

The Flow of Happiness.

Chapter 9 Sober Mindset.

When I was drinking every day, I truly believed that I was "treating myself". Wine was my reward, was what I was working towards each day. That first glass of wine punctuated the end of my working day and the beginning of adult relaxation time...never mind that the Wine Punctuation, if you like, was happening earlier and earlier every day!

Wine was my self-care, and it was a standing joke in my household that if my husband were considering making a romantic gesture, he should purchase wine rather than flowers. When I look back, that fills me with sadness for the woman I used to be, who chose poison over flowers

So when I quit, and I first encountered this concept of 'self-care" my thought process around it was something like..."*oh no, I've spent thousands of dollars, selfishly indulging my wine habit, and there's no way I am going to replace that with another self-indulgent practice – no, I deserve a life of deprivation to make up for all the decadence of my wine years"*

I didn't get it for a while. I had to really challenge my twisted logic, that wine was never a form of self- care or self- indulgence, it was a systematic method of self- destruction.

Instead of *adding* value, wine stripped away everything that is TRULY precious, my self-esteem, my moral compass, my integrity and my creativity. I had stopped loving myself, hell, I had stopped liking myself...at all! I avoided looking in the mirror when I washed my hands, I avoided checking my reflection, loathing my puffy features, my bloated silhouette.

It took a massive shift in my mindset to start looking after myself properly. To believing that I was worth looking after.

Baby steps at first. Once I had put down the bottle, I paid more attention to what my body needed. Sleep, exercise, good food and water.

I focused on addition, not elimination. You might find this yourself, it takes practice to everyday remind yourself that quitting drinking is not a deprivation, it's an act of love – so immediately initiating a strict diet, or imposing an exercise regime may seem like an extra punishment. At least it did to me, so I ate the ice cream and gradually added healthy stuff – an extra salad, or piece of fruit, until eventually, I didn't need the sugar anymore.

I was astounded at the almost immediate results.

Just about a month after I quit drinking, my Stepson and daughter-in-law Julie came to visit.

"You look awesome!" Julie said "You got rid of the plaid shirt and put something pretty on!"

Motivation to keep going is easier once you see some results – and it's contagious too!

On Day 28 I wrote:

"*So we have tried something that I have always regarded as slightly ridiculous, and only for the "health nuts' among us - juicing.*

Yes, we have consumed green juice, squished out from half a ton of kale. Ok, that's an exaggeration.

Actually, we have juiced our way through almost ten times the amount of veg and fruit that we usually consume. We have substituted two meals a day with fresh juice, and eat a healthy meal with a mountain of salad for the third.

The result? Well I have lost 12 pounds in the last four weeks (some of it undoubtedly due to being AF) and my husband has lost 17 pounds.

Now, as well as my obsession with sober blogs, sober memoirs and documentaries about alcohol, my husband is now just as obsessive about food....."Did you see how much sugar is in this?"....waving a jar of peanut butter furiously at me...."Are they TRYING to kill us? "(Loud voice in supermarket)....."Don't eat that cereal

!".......(To his bewildered grandson)....."You'll end up diabetic!" This summer we might just be the most boring couple alive!"

Stories and Ghosts.

We all tell ourselves stories. We tell ourselves stories about our failing, our flaws, about what other people think about us, about what terrible things might happen in our future because of our failings. We get so mired down in our stories, that we believe them, they become part of our identity, and they become self –filling prophecies.

The stories become our reality, because we *believe* them. And then we act on them.

Twelve years ago, I emigrated to Canada. I was in a long term relationship, which would ultimately fall apart, after we had been living in Canada for about three years.

Looking back, I can see now, that the relationship was showing all the signs of failing, long before we decided to make a "fresh start". In doing so, we managed to successfully distract ourselves for a period of time. The excitement of making this momentous decision, the application for Visas, medical checks, selling the house, shipping over our stuff, deciding where to live, all the "nuts and bolts' of upending our entire lives from one side of the world to the other.

Some couples, when they sense the cracks in their partnership, either plan a wedding or have a baby. We did neither. We emigrated. We attempted a *geographical cure.*

Three years later, when the dust settled, we were back to square one, same resentments, same distance, same infuriating noise when he chewed.......we hadn't fixed anything at all.

We began to believe that the relationship would fail. My partner so believed that I would eventually leave, that he began to behave in such a way to me, as if I were already leaving. He became angry and suspicious, he questioned my every move, he was miserable to be around.

I'm sure that I became distant.

Emotionally we were preparing ourselves for the end of the relationship. And began behaving like strangers towards each other. Eventually I did leave. There was no way the relationship would work. Our "story" became reality.

After fifteen years we just couldn't walk it back. The story instead became a self- fulfilling prophecy.

So we have to be careful of validating our stories to ourselves. If we are constantly telling ourselves that we are failures, we are not enough, we aren't smart enough, not responsible, whatever our story may be....it impacts the way we behave, and becomes a viscous circle.

We have to learn to validate our stories.

Is this real? Is this story true? Who told me this story and are they a reliable source?

Analyse it. Fact check it.

So many of our stories come from snatched snippets of conversations or misunderstandings, or misinterpreted *feelings*.

'Why didn't they call me? They must be mad with me. I bet they are still mad about that time when I (insert crime), and now they don't want anything to do with me..."

When the reality is that they are busy. Or they went on holiday.

Remember what my mum told me?

"No one is LOOKING AT YOU"

Affirmations.

OK, I'm not really a big fan of this.

Standing in front of a mirror in the morning whispering

"You are beautiful, you are strong, you are debt free..."

Augusten Burroughs wrote

"Affirmations are the psychological equivalent of sprinkling baby powder on top of the turd your puppy has left on the carpet. This does not result in cleaner carpet. It costs the underlying issue with futility"

Unfortunately for all of us, if we truly want to heal, we have to spend some time wading through the noxious swamp that spawned our intense self-hatred. In the first place.

And that involves visiting our past. Our most 'cringe worth moments". The type of memories that usually present themselves at three o'clock in the morning, or side swipe us at the most unexpected times.

Just before I quit drinking, my stepson bought us a bottle of wine. It was a really good bottle. "To drink", he said "when we celebrate our first purchase order for our fledgling business".

My husband was away for a couple of days. That bottle sung to me. And of course I drunk it all alone one night, despising myself for every mouthful, but seemingly powerless to stop.

The next morning I panicked. I searched all the liquor stores in town, and then drove to the next town, before I finally found the same bottle. $80. I had no choice. I paid, and took it home. I put it back on the rack.

Then, I remembered the empty bottle from the night before. What to do with it? I couldn't put it in the recycling, in case my husband found it.....

I hid it right at the back of the junkiest of our kitchen cupboards.

That was over a year ago.

I found it the other day. A physical reminder, like a punch in the gut.

In these instances, we need more than some cute sentences in front of our affirmation mirror.

We need a strategy that will allow us to reconcile ourselves with the past, and allow us to move on, feeling secure in our own skin.

My solution?

Embrace your messy past! Hug it to your bosom!

And then let it go.

Every step I took on the pathway of my life, whether it was clambering over rocks, or tumbling into valleys, taught me something.

Bruises fade, but the lessons stay. In that way, I can learn from the past, but I don't LIVE in the past.

Just One Rule at A Time.

When I moved to Canada from the UK in 2004, one of the major adjustments I faced (apart from a WHOLE DIFFERENT LANGUAGE cunningly disguised as English), was driving on the 'wrong" side of the road.

It was terrifying. When I first arrived in Vancouver, I avoided driving because of the handy Skytrain, but as

I ultimately wanted to live on Vancouver Island, it was evident really quickly, that I would have to take the plunge and drive.

I purchased a standard (stick shift) rather than an automatic. Why? *No freaking idea. The automatic would have been a whole lot easier.*

Instead, I struggled with changing gear with the wrong hand, setting off the wipers instead of the indicators, trying to get used to road signs..."Stop" instead of "Give Way", traffic lights that made no sense, being able to turn right on a red light, and absence of roundabouts.......*all on the wrong side of the road.*

To add insult to injury, I had to take another driving test, *twenty years after my first one – which included parallel parking!*

Thankfully I passed.

And now, eleven years later, it's as natural as breathing. I don't think about it. *99.99999% of the time.*

But very occasionally, I have a brain fart, and I try to get in the passenger side of my car to drive, or I find myself at an intersection, and for a split second....*I panic about being on the wrong side of the road!*

I tell myself;

'I am the driver. And the driver side is nearest the middle of the road. If I'm in the middle of the road – I am where I'm supposed to be".

And instantly I am fine. And so I go on, driving away, not thinking about it at all. Until the next brain fart happens.

Brain Farts Happen in Sobriety Too.

I am often asked if I still have a craving for wine, or if I think about drinking. And my answer is 'No....99.999% of the time".

And then, very occasionally, I find myself overcome with a *brain fart...and I want a glass of wine in my hand....*

But I have a rule.

I tell myself .....”You are a non-drinker. So you don't need or want a glass of wine. You are where you are supposed to be”

A simple statement that clears my mind – gives me a bit of a mental shake- and the craving goes.

Keep It Simple...

In early sobriety, there is so much to think about. Should I drink NA beer or wine? Should I count days? Am I in the middle of a pink cloud? What strategy should I use for the birthday party? *How do I handle this situation without booze?*

It can get really overwhelming. Much like re-learning how to drive.

Your life feels the same, except strangely awkward.

Then, you get used to it. You string a few days, weeks and months together. It feels OK. It feels familiar.

You are changing gear and parallel parking without thinking about it.

And then the brain fart. You look down, and there's no glass in your hand. You feel out of place. *On the wrong side of the road.*

Apply the rule...

Just. One. Rule.

Don't get distracted by flashing indicators, drivers honking behind you.......just slow right down...

Say to yourself...."I'm a non-drinker. I'm where I'm supposed to be"

And keep on driving.

Waiting Until You are Ready.

Maybe you are reading this with a glass of wine in your hand.

Oh, don't look so "shocked' – I read sober memoirs and self- help books while I was drinking too.

I was flirting with sobriety.

You know, until I was *ready.*

Such Bullshit.

Of course you're not ready. None of us ever is ready for a big lifestyle change. And that's the problem with readiness – we expend an awful lot of energy on 'getting ready" rather than just getting on with it.

Getting ready is really another way of describing procrastination. And procrastination, in these situations is really another version of FEAR.

We are basically afraid of making the change and therefore we keep telling ourselves that we are just waiting until we are ready.

And it is quite convenient. After all, there are thousands of well- meaning people out there who will tell you comfortingly – don't worry, you'll do this when you are READY.

As if one day, there will be a bolt of lightning, and you'll wake up READY for a sober life. In fact, I get several messages every week from people who tell me something similar....I wish I could wake up and not want to drink, which is basically the same as saying ...I wish I were READY for a sober life.

And this is understandable. After all, committing to a lifestyle transformation – maybe working through some quite unpleasant craving experiences, and also doing a lot of self –awareness work – examining those dark regions of our mind and dusting off a few memories that we prefer to leave in the shadows – is not the light, dancing with unicorns, sparkly experience that so many life style gurus would have you believe.

It's gritty. It's unpleasant. You come face to face with those parts of you that you hoped no-one would find - out, and you hoped you could bury.

So it's no wonder we put it off, until that magical day when we are ready.

We make lots of excuses like this;

Not until after the wedding. Or the summer. Or our anniversary.

The truth is, the best time to do ANYTHING is now...

Here's a great quote from Hugh Laurie

"It's a terrible thing, I think, in life to wait until you're ready. I have this feeling now that actually no one is ever ready to do anything. There is almost no such thing as ready. There is only now. And you may as well do it now. Generally speaking, now is as good a time as any"

My lesson here, is this – if you are worried about your drinking, then stop. Don't question it, if it bothers you, it is a problem. Don't try to measure your drinking against anyone else's, the quantity isn't important, the negative impact on your life is. Stop now. You're not ready. You never will be. It isn't going to be easy – there's no negotiating the first part, you just have to do it. You will NEVER wake up not wanting to drink, until you have experienced sobriety, and you have come to cherish it. When that happens, and if you do the work, it will.....I promise you that THEN, and only then, will you wake up never wanting to touch alcohol again.

Chapter 10 Sober Ever After

Imagine an elevator. At the top floor, people wander on and off the elevator, drinking occasionally, maybe getting drunk once in a while.

Maybe this is how you used to drink.

Go a few floors down, and you find the weekend binge drinkers. Carry on down further, the daily maintenance drinkers find it almost impossible to get off the elevator.

The further you travel down the elevator, the harder it is to return to the top floors.

For a short window of opportunity, some of us manage to 'reset" our relationship with alcohol and successfully moderate consumption. Some people can travel upwards.

But I am not one of them.

I do not believe that "Alcoholism" is a disease, I believe that abuse of alcohol is learned behaviour.

I learned early on, that alcohol provides temporary relief (or numbness) from stress. Many people have learned that booze is a shortcut to relaxing.

But here's the thing – all learned behaviour can be "unlearned"

It may be not easy, it may take some time, but with effort, diligence and gratitude, you can learn to live and thrive without booze.

If you do not, and you continue to ride the elevator down, at some point, you'll find that the "up" button simply isn't there anymore.

No one ever intends to ride the elevator down. No one ever intended to end up at the bottom floor. So if you feel that your drinking is out of control – NOW is good time to press the "stop" button.

Language and how we use it matters to me a great deal. I don't think we notice that very much, but remember when you were drinking? Or listen to people who are still drinking, how often do they say (or did you say) I really NEED a drink.

It seems a small thing but the words that repeatedly come out of our mouths are not only a product of our thoughts, they also serve to reinforce our thoughts and beliefs.

So while saying "I need a drink" may seem an innocuous remark – repeating that reinforces the notion until you no longer just WANT a drink you DO actually need it.

When I quit drinking, I was bothered by labels. I didn't want to be "an alcoholic in recovery" I wanted to be a non-drinker. So the language mattered to me.

I didn't want to be "in recovery" – I wanted to be cured. And I wanted to progress through to the point when I didn't feel like I was limited by drinking or not drinking – it simply isn't going to be a factor.

Many people follow a 12 Step program and achieve this.

But "steps" or moving through "steps" implies to me a linear program – at least that's the visual that I get. And I don't feel that my journey is linear.

It feels like I've been going round and round in circles sometimes. Or I've taken a detour to sort an issue out and I've doubled back occasionally. It has never felt like *a straight line.*

I studied psychology years ago.

During my studies, I came across many psychologists (many whom I'm revisiting now – you see what I mean about detours and doubling back?) but for this VISUAL of my sober quest – Abraham Maslow turned out to be my guy.

Abraham Maslow came up with the concept of Maslow's Hierarchy of Human Needs. Picture a pyramid. At the base of the pyramid of needs is all the stuff we need for basic survival. Food, water, shelter, without this stuff, we don't need anything else because we won't make it. Then once these needs are met, we look around for security because we need to feel safe.

 Moving up the pyramid, we come to Love and Belonging – our social needs. Our human need to feel accepted into some kind of a group. Then, once we feel part of something, we can satisfy our need to elevate our self- esteem – to feel good about ourselves. ONLY then can we fulfil our need (according to Maslow) for self- actualization – basically to fulfil what we perceive as our purpose in life. Achieving our highest human potential.

Much later, after completing this pyramid, Maslow added the pinnacle to human needs – transcendence – our spirituality, our altruism.

Now, it can be argued that this only works to a point – because, or course, we can feel spiritual, even when starving – humans are very complex and don't fit as neatly into this pyramid, and Maslow was criticised for not paying attention to any gender difference, or changes in humans situations – but you get the idea, that, in general, when we are scrambling around to SURVIVE – we are probably not paying much attention to our self-esteem. And until we are fed and watered, we are probably not thinking about living to our fullest potential.

I like this pyramid, this building on a foundation of needs. Not only does it visually appeal to me, I find it helpful to view my sober journey, as building on a foundation. Each stage is a new platform to master before I move on up to the next.

At the bottom of the pyramid is what we need to master for our sober survival – overcoming our fears and denial, the sober strategies that we need to employ – all the sober tools at our disposal – meetings, blogging, the *basics* of sobriety.

We build on this foundation. We learn to socialize without an alcoholic drink in our hand. We deal with our daily issues and problems without reaching for the bottle. We rebuild relationships, we develop our creativity and finally we transcend.

Higher Power.

Early on in my sobriety, I fled into my garden and started weeding furiously to escape the Wine Witch.

It worked.

So I did it again the next evening. And then again.

I had cleared quite a patch – and then my husband gently explained that they weren't all weeds....so we spent an hour re-planting.

And then I was hooked.

Since then I have acquired a greenhouse. Someone was throwing it away, and my husband rescued it and re-built it for me. He built me EIGHT raised beds. And then a Gazebo. Last year was my best harvest so far (although I couldn't figure out the problem with my tomatoes and I did grow about fifty pumpkins...who knew they would all "take"?) and this year I am being far more adventurous.

Now, instead of a bottle of wine, my husband brings me new plants...A Miniature Kiwi! Raspberry Bushes! A Lemon Tree! I am giddy with delight.

Every morning, I check to see how my seedlings are doing, with my coffee in my hand. In the evenings, with dirt under my nails, I have my tea, under my Gazebo.

Life has changed. I have changed. I'm more concerned about the planet and our environment (never crossed my mind while I was drinking), I think about *stuff when I am planting.* I feel more connected and yet "freer" if that makes any sense at all.

Time stands still when I'm in the greenhouse. I am literally *grounded.*

I finally found my Higher Power. He was waiting in the garden.

If you needed any more Motivation....

I would hazard a guess, and say that most of us don't feel very powerful, and lots of us don't feel very "free". Freedom and power seem to be very subjective concepts.

However we choose to live our lives, we do so within the confines of the circumstances into which we are born, and the opportunities that are open to us, and our ability to recognise and act upon those opportunities.

Many of us feel that whatever we do, whatever limited choices we make in our lives – we cannot and do not make an impact on the world, and are unable to change our circumstances, HOWEVER many times we are told that we are free.

But we do have one last freedom left. And this FREEDOM, does, I believe TRULY empower us, TRULY gives us political clout, and can TRULY change the world.

It's the FREEDOM to choose what we physically consume.

You may not think you are a political person, but by choosing NOT to consume alcohol, you are also removing support from a powerful group of corporations who constantly misrepresent basically "flavoured poison" as fun and harmless, who intentionally perpetuate the "myth" of the alcoholic as a person who is either diseased, or psychologically damaged, or weak, in order to convince the rest of the population that drinking booze is OK.

You are also removing your support from an industry that is actively looking to expand its markets and hence it profits by targeting younger and younger consumers, parents, and even invading the recovery space, by working with the fitness industry. All for profit. You are removing support from the industry that uses it's considerably deep pockets to challenge any and all increases in taxes and regulations because it's worried that governments might put the health of its citizens before free market mechanisms that are driven solely by profit.

By choosing NOT to participate, YOU are taking your power back – and using that free market mechanism against them.

The FREEDOM to choose what we consume also impacts the environment.

You may not think of yourself as an environmental activist – but by choosing NOT to consume alcohol, you are removing support from the wine industry for example that prefers to portray itself as "natural", and working with "nature"

You've seen all those pictures of rolling hills covered in vines, dappled sunlight, and happy workers plucking plump grapes ready to make into wine…*an age old craft steeped in tradition*

The reality is that most vineyards and wineries use upwards of 50 different chemical pesticides (in France, there are many pending lawsuits from Wine Industry workers whose health has been adversely affected by pesticide use – France uses upwards of 60,000 tonnes of pesticides per year). Every day, these pesticides leech into the earth affecting out ground water supply, and eventually making their way into our oceans. The growing "dead zone" areas in our oceans caused directly by agriculture, that includes the alcohol industry – means that by 2050, our oceans will be virtually fish-free.

And what are about the grain based alcohol products – what indeed? In a world where 3 billion people are starving, we dedicate over 50% of grain produced for non – food products, which includes ethanol production. A large majority of that grain production is genetically modified – and no one knows the long term impact of that on our health, or our environment.

And if that's not enough, by stopping drinking, you will have personally affected the over- consumption of water, an increasingly valuable resource, as we are now experiencing drought on a world wide scale that we have never before seen in the modern era.

So if you think that by quitting drinking, you are not making any impact on our world – you're wrong! By exercising your freedom to NOT consume alcohol – you ARE changing the world.

Lastly, you may think that your personal choice to not consume booze, would only affect YOUR bank account.

But that is incorrect. You are impacting the economy in a positive way. By showing up to work clearheaded and focused and by not taking those spurious sick days, your productivity has increased, and you are thereby directly affecting the efficiency of the organisation you work for. Or maybe you've questioned your calling, and have started a new career or business.

If you are a "soberpreneur" you will be single -handed contributing to the economy (small businesses are the life blood of every economy)

By having more cash in your pocket, you can choose to spend this disposable income on products and businesses that align with your values, that are able to increase employment, and raise the standard of living – rather than dump your cash into alcohol corporations that line the pockets of the few.

And think about this – when we feel empowered, when we feel that we're making a difference, when we feel part of society, when we can pay our bills....we're not living in fear, and blame, and scarcity and survival mode – we're not fearful of our neighbours who may have a different colour skin, or worship a different God, or eat different food, or dress differently....

Your decision to not drink, to NOT pick up the bottle...is like dropping a tiny pebble into a pond, the ripples keep expanding outwards and outwards...

You are EMPOWERED, you DO make a difference, you CAN change the world...

Your sobriety is no longer a destination.

Your sobriety is a tool that empowers you to live your life to your fullest potential, to set an example to your kids and your peers, and to impact the world around you in a positive way.

That's what I think.

That why I am Sober Ever After.

The "How To" Resources

I wish I could write a definitive How – To Guide for Quitting Booze.

But what worked for me, might not work for you. In sober circles, it's common to hear the phrase;

'There is no One Size Fits All approach to sobriety"

Some people may need the support of a group environment, others may find the relatively anonymous on-line community a better or more convenient fit.

Many people find that a spiritual approach works well, and others find that a more psychological cognitive perspective makes more sense.

I basically "cherry-picked" from them all. And then tweaked and adjusted as I progressed

As a self-confessed "girl of science", the traditional AA model didn't resonate with me at first. I preferred the teaching of my Psychology background. But then I found that it was almost impossible for me to grow and develop my self- awareness without acknowledging that something *spiritual was happening too.*

Here's what I discovered to be universally true, from my own experience and from all those inspirational people that I've had to privilege of meeting along the way.

You need to Pay Attention.

Some of the things that I declared *most emphatically* to be true, at the beginning of this journey...I view in a different way now. I've read blogs, novels, self-help books, essays, medical reports and research. And some have given me insight and advice, but NOTHING has been a substitute for my own experience. And the first thing I have learned.....is PAY ATTENTION. Pay attention to what you feel. Pay attention to what your body tells you. One thing that we DON"T do when we are drinking, is pay attention to ourselves and our reactions.

If someone is making you feel uncomfortable, pay attention to that feeling. If a particular activity or sober strategy that someone has suggested doesn't feel right...pay attention to that feeling.

Some people call it navel gazing.

I call it ...*essential.*

Take Action, But Only for Today.

Today, eat healthily. Today, take some exercise. Today, complete a couple of things on your To-Do list. Today, start a project, or de-clutter a cupboard. Today, make sure you get to bed early. Today, say a prayer, or meditate.

Don't. Drink. Today.

Don't Carry Other People's Baggage.

I once had a partner who was scornful and mocking of his elder sister when she discovered the spiritual side of herself.

"Just look at her, with a stupid smile on her face, acting like she has this big secret, if she's better than us, because she suddenly found God"

I've had variations of this attitude since I quit. It comes in many forms....direct attacks, passive aggressive behaviour like trying to pick a fight, arriving at your house with wine...

Don't try to explain. Don't make excuses for yourself. Don't engage in their drama.

It's their baggage. Don't carry it for them.

Conversely, I have strengthened and renewed relationships. I've found friendship and support in unexpected places.

If you want to find out who your friends are....get sober!

Don't Be a Victim

I fully accept that I have no control over alcohol.

But I don't have to surrender my power to alcohol.

We all have our different, important and valid reasons for picking up the bottle.

But, (unless there are truly horrible circumstances), no-one held a gun to our head and forced us to drink.

So, at some point, we have to be accountable to ourselves for that decision.

And until you do, you are going to continuously "bump" into your drunken past.

I caught glimpses of myself at parties. I lay awake re-living some of the things that I said, wrote, posted and gossiped about.

Even though we were under the influence of Alcohol – we are still responsible for the impact of our behaviour.

Take the chance to apologise if it's possible.

Not only will you take your power back, it's the right thing to do.

We are all Unique...But Mostly the Same.

None of us are special.

Lots of us are lucky *that it didn't get much worse..*

But none of us are special.

If you hear yourself saying...

Oh but I can't give up because of...............................(insert "special circumstances")

or

It's much harder for me because of..........................(insert "special circumstances")

Then you are hearing Alcohol speaking to you.

You are not special. I am not special. The path goes in the same direction for all of us.

This means that counting days may not work for you. It means that drinking AF beer may not work for you. It may mean that AA meetings work or don't work for you.

There may not be a 'blanket approach" for everyone, but,

Everyone is journeying in the same direction.

Some Resources.

- Visit http://www.aa.org/ to find an AA meeting near you, or download resources.

- Visit http://www.smartrecovery.org/ to find (or start!) a SMART Recovery Group in your community.

- Visit https://www.iamrunningonsober.com/for articles, podcasts, blogs and access to online programs.

Blogs I Love.

- http://livingwithoutalcohol.blogspot.ca/ Mrs. D is Going Without. Catch up on her latest blog and also get access to many sober bloggers around the globe.

- http://mummywasasecretdrinker.blogspot.ca/

- https://godwalkedintothisbar.blogspot.ca/

- http://quitwining.com/

- http://www.lauramckowen.com/

This is not an exhaustive list. The great thing about the Sober Online Community is that when you start following one blogger, they will direct you to other superb bloggers.

You may want to start your own blog – please do! It's an excellent way to keep accountable and build your 'sober tribe'!

Enjoy this book? You can make a big difference

Reviews are the most powerful tool I have when it comes to getting attention for my books. Much as I'd like to, I can't take out full page ads in the newspaper or put posters on billboard to spread the sober message!

(Not yet, anyway)

But I do have something much more powerful and effective.

A committed and loyal bunch of readers.

Honest reviews of my books help bring them to the attention of other readers, and who knows? It might just be at the right time, when someone needs a bit more motivation to carry on their sober journey.

If you have enjoyed this book, I would be really grateful if you would leave a review on the book's Amazon page.

You can just click below. Thank you so much.

US

UK

CA

Get a FREE Ebook !

Building a relationship with my readers is the very best thing about writing. I send newsletters with details on new releases, links to my blogs and podcasts, and articles.

You can also grab a copy of my FREE ebook when you visit my website:

www.iamrunningonsober.com

Also By Jackie Elliott

How I Quit Drinking (and how you can too)

Feeling stuck in the drinking spiral? Tried to moderate, but fail every time? Tired of waking up with low level hangover every day, sick of your "booze boobs" and lack of energy?

Quitting drinking is HARD. And worse than that, you feel all alone, because the WHOLE WORLD loves booze!

But you know you have to do something. It's getting worse, and you are felling out of control. You are frightened that you'll end up as an.......*alcoholic (whispers)*

Jackie was in the exact same place. And wrote this book for YOU, to guide you through your sober journey *without going to any meetings if you don't want to!*

This book is a road map. It doesn't hold the 'secret short cut' to sobriety, because there are none, but it does sign-post you through the "getting sober" and guide you towards "living sober" (two very different things).

This book is full of practical guidance for all the phases of the sober journey – what to do when your first pink cloud dissipates, how do you prepare for your first sober outing, why aren't your friends cheering you on? What's up with that?

And when do you actually get to BE sober? And is there life beyond this journey – in the scary new non-drinking world?

This book acknowledges that this journey is dual purpose – to ditch the booze and find oneself – and the power and success of recovery comes when you can use sobriety as a tool in your life, rather than a destination. Everybody has a unique sober journey – but everyone's path goes in the same direction. This book will help you get there, hopefully without too many detours.

How I Quit Drinking (and how you can too) is a practical, helpful (and sometimes humorous) guide from an award winner blogger, who ploughed her own sober path and made it through!

If you have had enough of being slave to the Wine Witch, buy this book today, and transform your life!

Dedication:

For my patient husband Bob, who always supports me, no matter what, and the Sober Blogging Community

Jackie Elliott.

Jackie lives on Vancouver Island, with her husband and cat. You can find her online home at www.iamrunningonsober.com and follow her on Facebook or Instagram

Copyright.

CPSIA information can be obtained
at www.ICGtesting.com
Printed in the USA
BVHW041214211119
564177BV00018BB/1396/P